Plagiarism in *Writing*

REAL LANGUAGE SERIES

General Editors:

JENNIFER COATES, Roehampton Institute, London

JENNY CHESHIRE, Queen Mary and Westfield College, University of London, and

EUAN REID, Institute of Education, University of London

Stolen Language?
Plagiarism in Writing

Shelley Angélil-Carter

An imprint of **Pearson Education**

Harlow, England · London · New York · Reading, Massachusetts · San Francisco · Toronto · Don Mills, Ontario · Sydney
Tokyo · Singapore · Hong Kong · Seoul · Taipei · Cape Town · Madrid · Mexico City · Amsterdam · Munich · Paris · Milan

Pearson Education Limited
Edinburgh Gate
Harlow
Essex CM20 2JE
England

and Associated Companies throughout the world

Visit us on the World Wide Web at:
www.pearsoneduc.com

First published 2000

© Pearson Education Limited 2000

ISBN 0–582–31998–6 CSD
ISBN 0–582–31999–4 PPR

British Library Cataloguing-in-Publication Data
A catalogue record for this book is available from the British Library

Library of Congress Cataloging-in-Publication Data
Angélil-Carter, Shelley.
  Stolen Language? : plagiarism in writing / Shelley Angélil-Carter.—2nd ed.
    p. cm. — (Real language series)
  Includes bibliographical references and index.
  ISBN 0–582–31998–6 — ISBN 0–582–31999–4 (pbk.)
    1. Plagiarism. 2. Imitation in literature. 3. Literary ethics. I. Title. II. Series.
PN167.A64 2000
  808—dc21   99–087296

Set in 10/12pt Janson by 35
Produced by Pearson Education Asia Pte Ltd.
Printed and bound by Antony Rowe Ltd, Eastbourne

Contents

For my parents, Arthur
and Roma Carter,
with love and gratitude

Acknowledgements

Although this work was authored by me, this is a multivoiced text, in that there were many around me who helped me to think through the ideas presented here, and who gave me feedback on various drafts of this book. Here I would like to thank Lucia Thesen, Rob Moore, Rochelle Kapp, Moragh Paxton, Nadia Hartman, Cathy Hutchings, Tim Hughes, Suellen Shay, Dr Hilary Janks and Professor Paul Walters. Thanks also to Hilary Janks and Sarah Murray for their assistance and encouragement in getting this book published. My thanks go to the editors of the Real Language Series for supporting this book from the start, and particular thanks to Euan Reid for his gentle but insightful feedback, in guiding this book towards publication. The book would not have been possible without the participation of all the students, tutors and academic staff whom I interviewed, and I am grateful to them for sharing their writing, thoughts and ideas with me.

The work was supported by a grant from the University of Cape Town's University Research Committee, for which I would like to express my appreciation.

Special thanks are due to Sarah Murray, for her always generous sharing of her knowledge, for her accessibility and encouragement, and for generally acting as a very supportive midwife to this baby.

Finally I thank my husband, Serge Angélil, and my children, Raymond, Oliver and Lauren, for dancing with me.

1

Introduction: *an overture*

Academic staff often feel frustrated when students find academic referencing or citation difficult, and they are concerned about the prevalence of plagiarism. Generally referencing is seen by academic staff as a technical problem to which students need to apply their minds, whilst students (and teachers of academic literacy) find it a difficult problem to grapple with.

A letter to a University of Cape Town newspaper, the *Monday Paper*, responding to an article written by myself and Cathy Hutchings (1995), typifies some of the thinking about plagiarism:

> From the outset I must declare an interest in the subject of plagiarism as I frequently encounter it when having to mark undergraduate work. My position is clear, any piece of work that is not properly referenced will result in the student being penalised. I will not sanction the deliberate theft of another person's intellectual property. It is nothing short of outrageous to suggest that the protocols against plagiarism are merely part of some academic game. The suggestion that a student becomes so immersed in the subject that he/she is unable to differentiate between his/her own ideas and those gained from research is worthy of nothing but derision. Just as inflation is the scourge of a country's economy, so is plagiarism the scourge of academic life.
>
> (Letter to *Monday Paper*, 21–28 Aug. 1995)

The 'scourge of plagiarism' attitude will be a familiar one to many of those reading this book. Many academics spend hours attempting to ferret out the plagiarized source, feeling morally outraged and determined to find evidence for the crime. Plagiarism is seen as deceitful and dishonest, its perpetrators are fraudulent, and must be severely penalized. The language used is often about crime and investigation – 'perpetrators', 'theft', 'penalize' – and there seems to be perfect (unspoken) clarity on what constitutes 'intellectual property'.

Murphy (1990) describes the 'thrill' of the 'chase' to find the sources the student has copied from, prove the student's guilt, and have the student suspended from the university, as happened in one of the cases Murphy describes. Another of Murphy's students, whom he suspected of plagiarism in an essay about her own anorexia, when interrogated by Murphy, eventually said that the paper was not about herself, but about a friend. She was given zero on the paper, as Murphy had felt that it was a hoax, and still suspected plagiarism. At the end of the semester, when Murphy collected her journal, he came across journal entries which were clearly sincere, and which indicated that the anorexia experience, as well as the essay, had been the student's own. Murphy's own bewilderment at what had happened is clear: he was 'astonished and appalled' (903) and ends his article with the words, 'I did not mean for it to come to this' (903). How did it come to this? Why is plagiarism considered such a heinous crime that some academics will spend hours in the library chasing up possible source material, and students will deny their own experience when suspected of plagiarism? What kinds of students, what kinds of writing cause academics to suspect plagiarism? Murphy calls it 'an intuition, some feeling on the surface of the page, something about the dye of the ink that whispers this is counterfeit currency; the excitement of judicial self-satisfaction' (900). What makes up this 'intuition', and how accurate is it? Why do students plagiarize, and what exactly can be counted as plagiarism?

There is no sense in the letter quoted above that plagiarism could be anything other than 'deliberate theft of another person's intellectual property'. What I hope to establish in this book is that plagiarism in the undergraduate years is not so much a matter of 'deliberate theft', though this of course occurs, but is rather a complex problem of student learning, compounded by a lack of clarity about the concept of plagiarism itself, and a lack of clear policy and pedagogy surrounding the issue. Plagiarism is a 'naturalized' concept which seems unquestioned by those who enforce its discipline. Citation is also a 'naturalized' skill, so central to academic writing that much of its complexity is never made explicit.

Plagiarism is in fact a modern Western construct which arose with the introduction of copyright laws in the eighteenth century. Before this time, there was little sense of artistic 'ownership'. Since then, the idea of 'originality' in writing has been highly valued. The analysis presented in this book will show that plagiarism is a complex, contested concept, and in student academic writing it may be the surface manifestation of complex learning difficulties which relate to the educational environment, the nature of academic discourse and the nature of language.

Underlying the concept of plagiarism is the basic premise that meaning is made by the individual, using the system of language at his or her disposal. The words and ideas thus originated then belong to the individual who first thought of them, or who first used these words in a particular way. New understandings, that language and cognition are fundamentally social and cultural, contest the idea of 'original thought' or 'original language'.

In this book, however, I attempt to show that although the concept of authorship is under attack in postmodern thought, along with the notion of agency, there *is* in any writing an *agent, an authorial presence*. The presence of authorial voice in academic writing is particularly difficult for the student writer to accomplish when constructing an essay based on multiple texts.

I shall show that plagiarism is an elusive concept, difficult to define, meaning different things in different contexts and for different textual genres. My principal interest in writing this book is to understand what plagiarism means in the context of academic writing, and to explore what may be happening when a student writer is thought to be plagiarizing. The primary aim of this exploration, with the help of a theoretical framework and with the insights gained from interviewing students and staff and analysing writing, is to understand plagiarism differently. The secondary objective, which this book attempts to fulfil, is to find ways of communicating this new understanding to those who teach others how to become writers of academic discourse, and to writers of academic discourse.

The context: *the social practice of language in academic development*

Much of my thinking and exploration of plagiarism began when I was a lecturer in language development in the Academic Development Programme (ADP) at the University of Cape Town (UCT). The ADP began as the Academic Support Programme (ASP) in the early 1980s, to develop 'bridging' programmes for black students, inadequately prepared due to poor schooling, coming onto a campus which traditionally had catered mainly to white students from well-resourced schools. Particularly inadequate education was provided in schools run by the infamous Department of Education and Training (DET), which was the structure set up by the apartheid government to administer schooling to African children.[1]

One of the early courses set up by the ASP was an English for Academic Purposes course, which concentrated on 'bridging' for the Arts and Social Sciences, and in other faculties many other foundation courses and supplementary tutorials followed. In the early 1990s, it became clear that the university did not have the resources to support growing numbers of black students in these programmes, and that the university itself was inadequately prepared for enabling the potential of all its students to be fulfilled. The focus of the ASP began to turn from students to learning environments, concentrating on staff and curriculum development to cater for student diversity, whilst still retaining the support structures, and the ASP became the Academic Development Programme. A Writing Centre was set up to provide writing development consultations for all students, as well as to work with academic departments across the curriculum.

Within this context, we had encountered great difficulty with the practice of citation or referencing in academic writing in our teaching of English for Academic Purposes, and in the experience of the Writing Centre. For several years we had realized that there is much more to citation than simply understanding the technical details of how to write the author's name, when to write the page number and how to present a complete bibliography in an academic essay. We understood citation as the superficial manifestation of a much deeper, elemental feature of academic writing, which is the analysis of and selection from sources, and subsequent integration and synthesis of knowledge and ideas into a coherent whole.

Discourse and reflexivity: *writing honest but guilty text*

> to write 'postmodern' is to write paradoxically aware of one's complicity in that which one critiques.
>
> (LATHER, 1991: 10)

My 'complicity' in what I shall critique in this book is deep. While writing academic discourse, I shall be critiquing it. While investigating the multivoiced text, I shall be writing one. While attempting to deconstruct such notions as 'plagiarism', I shall often feel like a thief. Crucially, I am intensely aware of the extent to which my meaning is a construction of the meanings of many others: those I read, those I live with, work with, the staff and students I interviewed for this book. Some of them I am able to acknowledge, and some not. Of some of my words I do not know the origin, but they have never been only 'mine'. Like Lather, I see some way out of this dilemma of critique/collaboration by trying to be as self-consciously reflexive as possible of my stances and positions.

The way in which I choose to write this book is to remain within a recognizable discourse of language in education, but to legitimate elements of an/other kind of discourse in academic writing. The principal way in which I do this is to use metaphor, in order to open up my thinking to the thoughts of others, and to provide unity and coherence. I make conscious use of metaphor (and unconscious, as we all do) throughout this book. Lakoff and Johnson (1980) argue convincingly that metaphors, often unperceived as metaphor, actually shape perception, thought and action. They demonstrate, for instance, how the metaphor of 'argument as war' structures how we think about argument, with expressions such as 'attack' and 'defend'. They posit a different culture where argument might be understood as dance (5), a metaphor which I shall use extensively, though differently, in this book. They suggest that in such a culture, where the aim of argument would be to demonstrate balance and beauty, people would think about argument differently, and would argue differently.

The word metaphor comes from the Greek 'metaphora' meaning 'to carry over' (Bowers and Flinders, 1990: 34). It allows us to carry over and apply one schematic frame to another, and this requires imagination and opens language up to multiple interpretations through symbol. I am very aware that metaphorical meanings are culturally based. Nevertheless I think the fact that dance, for example, means different things to different readers is part of the symbolic openness, and part of the power, of metaphor.

I wish to respect the notions of discourse which are developed in the next chapter, as fundamentally social and contextual, by encouraging the reader to reinterpret and recontextualize what I write. I invite others to dance with me, and to take my dance and make it their own.

Note

1. There were several other education structures: a department for whites, one for 'coloureds' (people of mixed race) and one for Asians, as well as Education Departments for each of the so-called 'homelands' of the apartheid system.

Dancing a Theoretical Stance

2

Discourses and access: *dancers in the wings*

I begin in this chapter with a theoretical framework for understanding plagiarism. In the sections following, I view my context through the lens of theories of discourse and genre, arguing that control of powerful discourses and the genres in which they are expressed is a crucial means of access.

The tacit nature of discourses: *tribal dances*

Bourdieu and Passeron (1994: 8) write that 'Academic language is a dead language for the great majority of French people, and is no one's mother tongue'. Though I believe that academic discourse is very much alive within the borders of its social context, Bourdieu and Passeron's point is that it is something that has to be learned, as it is not anybody's home language. It is also a discourse which is closer to the home-based discourses of particular groups, and therefore in itself perpetuates differential success rates within the university. They argue that democratizing the academy not only means granting access into the institution to those who are not 'children of the cultivated classes'. (8) Success within the institution means also that the exclusive nature of academic discourse has to be addressed, as it is crucial for success in examinations. They go on to say that if you define criteria for assessment and make a framework of expectations clear and explicit, you can significantly reduce the disadvantages of the 'disfavoured groups' (22) without favouring any group in particular. In other words, making the codes of academic discourse explicit has advantages for all students.

Academic discourses are deeply yet often unconsciously understood by those who practise them daily, i.e. academics. Ballard and Clanchy (1988) throw some light on the disjunctures, as represented by the letter quoted in Chapter 1, between academics and their students. For them academic literacy is 'a student's capacity to use written language to perform those functions required by the culture in ways and at a level judged acceptable by the reader' (8). Theirs is an anthropological conception of academic literacy, in that they see academic disciplines as 'cultures' where there is a fundamental link between 'the culture of knowledge and the language by which it is maintained and expressed' (7). The academics in a discipline, as full members of this culture, have a set of cultural understandings and codes, which the academics themselves know intimately but mostly unconsciously, and therefore seldom make explicit to students. Compounding this situation is Rose's concept of the 'myth of transience', where the 'writing problem' is seen as something transient which will go away 'if we can just do x or y' and then 'higher education will be able to return to its real work' (Rose, 1985: 355). This is a myth: academic literacy can only be achieved by engaging with the discipline, and writing is intimately related to disciplinary inquiry. Thus we need to understand a discipline as a culture with its own set of rules and behaviours, which is learnt best within the culture. Writing is an integral part of the way in which the culture is expressed, developed and maintained. This leads us to an understanding of why, unless the codes are explicitly taught, historically excluded students are at greater risk: their distance from the cultures which they seek to enter is greater than that of their advantaged peers.

Using the word 'culture' is one way of describing how institutions and social groupings have paricular social meanings and ideologies which are expressed in language in systematic ways. Following Kress (1985), I prefer to call these systematic ways of speaking or writing 'discourses'.

Discourse and access: *coming onstage*

Kress defines discourses as

> systematically-organized sets of statements which give expression to the meanings and values of an institution. . . . A discourse . . . provides descriptions, rules, permissions and prohibitions of social and individual actions.
>
> (1985: 7)

In Kress's definition, with phrases such as 'values of an institution', 'provides descriptions, rules, permissions and prohibitions', it is clear that discourses are ideologically based, and linked to power. Access to a privileged position in society requires that one acquires the privileged discourses of society. These are linked to social goods, and are unevenly distributed (Gee, 1990). Gee expresses the interrelationship between access and discourse as follows. He defines a person's 'primary Discourse' (with a capital D) as that 'which is developed in the primary process of enculturation' (151), and secondary Discourses as those which are developed outside of the home, in the church or the school, for example. For those whose primary Discourses are congruent to the Discourses of power, there are easier transitions, and easier access to social goods. For those whose primary Discourses are distant from the Discourses of power, the latter act as gatekeepers, and deny those who do not speak them access to social goods.

Academic discourse, like any other, is a social practice. In terms of success at the university, written academic discourse is extremely important, as it is most often the way in which students (and academics) are judged and evaluated. Academic discourse becomes a gatekeeper, denying access to social goods to those who do not succeed. In a post-apartheid South Africa, a substantial proportion of our students still come from poor educational backgrounds. Their primary discourses may be very different from that of the school, and these discourses may be substantially different from that of the university. Failure to make the transitions successfully is a real possibility. Reynolds and de Klerk (1998) use a model based on Gee's primary and secondary Discourses, considering the secondary Discourses of both the school and the university, formal and informal. To this they add the factor of the language medium used in these Discourses. They compare two students, and their academic success, and conclude that the student whose home and secondary Discourses were closer to and more valued by the university succeeded academically, while the other was unable to close the gaps and dropped out of his studies.

Shirley Brice Heath (1983) studied the home literacy practices in three different, geographically close communities in the USA. One was mainly middle-class (she called it Maintown), one was white and working-class (Roadville) and the third, Trackton, was a black working-class community. Her research uncovered significant differences in home literacy practices and how these are received in the classroom. Her findings were complex, but showed clearly how some of the home literacy practices (for example, the rich oral literacy practices of the Trackton community) were not as valued in the classroom as others.

Reynolds and de Klerk, and to some extent Gee, do not adequately take into account the notion of human agency, i.e. how the two students used the discourses that they brought to the university, and how they acted upon or failed to act upon the discourses they encountered. Thesen (1997) critiques the determinism inherent in Gee's (1990) view of a subject being either 'insider, colonized or an outsider' (155). Gee's notion of agency seems to be one which is at work within the rules of the discourse, rather than one which can challenge the rules themselves. Thesen understands individuals as very often aware of what discourse they are operating within, and her research shows people making strategic choices about which discourse in their repertoire to access and use. The central point that Thesen is making, that we have to take into account the power of the active agent in discourse theory, is one which is central to any work on authorship, and will be revisited throughout this book. The choreographer, with diverse dance styles in her repertoire, chooses to draw on those best suited to the piece she is creating, and considers the music, the dancers and the audience in her choice. She may create an entirely new dance style in so doing.

Agency must incorporate the notion of passive agency. Bourdieu and Passeron (1994) see professor and student as *complicit* in a relationship of misunderstanding of academic discourse, as both parties benefit from the pretence of a functioning communication. Those who refuse to engage with the discourses themselves, i.e. refuse to take them on and up, but choose to stand outside them in a rejection of what they stand for, are choosing a form of passive resistance which alienates but does not transform. If men see ballet as a feminine art form, and refuse to engage with it, there will be no transformation of ballet into a form in which both male and female are celebrated.

In Fairclough's work, human agency contributes to the struggles around discourse change. He sees within discourses the intense struggles around language, and in his work there is a sense of individuals both constrained and empowered by discourses (Fairclough, 1992). His understanding of discourse is a dialectical one: discourses are both constitutive and transformative of social practice. Thus the extent to which students are able to control academic discourse will partially determine the extent to which they can challenge it, and force it to open up to previously marginalized discourses, allowing different discourses in. The cakewalk, a strutting, high-stepping promenade, which satirized the haughty ways of plantation masters, was created by slaves in the American South. A new dance form was created as a form of resistance to the slave masters. By the 1890s it had become popular amongst high-society whites in the USA, and was practised as a mainstream social dance. Critique from the margins will impact on the dominant discourses.

Although Academic Development work focuses on access to dominant discourses, I like to think that the long-term goal is to empower students to reshape and remake those discourses. There is a risk in learning to dance too well to the tune of the dominant discourses, that you will be 'colonized' by that discourse (Gee, 1990), and not act to change it. Coming onstage is one step, dancing (perhaps with a critical eye) the dominant discourses another, and fusing a new form of expression is a further step, which may or may not follow.

Access and explicitness in genre theory:
taking the learner backstage

Genres are 'conventionalised forms of texts', which 'derive from and encode the functions, purposes and meanings of social occasions' (Kress, 1985: 19).

Discourses and genres overlap, but Kress distinguishes usefully between them: discourses have to do with larger social institutions, and carry their meanings, whilst genres refer to social events or occasions and the forms of text these occasions demand. So, for example, the institution of psychology has resulted in psychological discourse. This institution has its own social occasions organized into genres such as the psychotherapeutic interview, the conference paper, the workshop. A text will be determined both by the *discourse* of psychology, and by the particular *genre* demanded by the social occasion. The text which I am presenting now is informed by the discourses of Applied Linguistics, Academic Development, and Education, but its genre is that of a book for the use of academics, teachers and students, a genre which has a particular function in society. This genre can and does carry many other discourses.

Genre theorists such as Cope and Kalantzis (1993) criticize progressivist educational theorists who do not acknowledge that some genres are more powerful than others. They deride the postmodernist notion of 'difference', interpreting these theorists as arguing that 'there is no superior Western canon any more, only different literary and cultural traditions. . . . The notion that there might be a "standard" of correct English was only ever sheer prejudice' (1993: 5). Cope and Kalantzis's interpretation of these theorists can be contested, but the point they wish to make is that there *is* a powerful standard, there *is* a Western canon, there are powerful genres that are more highly valued than others and we ignore them to the detriment of those who do not 'naturally' have access to these genres. They argue against progressivist notions such as 'process writing' and 'voice', which emphasize individual creativity and 'difference' and simply further disadvantage those who are marginalized. The genre theorists, in general, make a plea for explicit teaching of powerful genres of writing, because without this, the control of these genres remains available only to those who are 'born' to them by virtue of the social milieus in which they live.

The genre approach has been criticized by literacy theorists such as Street (1995). He regards the notion of empowerment through making genres explicit as a simplification of the way in which power structures work. He writes:

> There is much research to be done yet on the actual relations between specific genres and the holding of power, financial and political. To lead students to believe that there is a one-way relationship between particular genres taught in school and those positions is to set them up for disappointment and disillusion.

> (140)

I think it is clear that there is no 'one-way relationship' between genres and positions of power: making genres explicit is only a small part of access to social goods. What the genre theorists have done is focus our attention on

how 'naturalized' many genres are, and in their 'natural', taken-for-granted form only available to certain groups of people. Street also believes that the genre approach of teaching students to control the dominant genres first, so that later they are able to critique them – he calls it the 'wait for critique' approach (139) – is 'fundamentally flawed and deeply conservative' (141), because literacy learning is about process as well as content. The learner needs to be taken through a *process* which exposes both *forms* of genres as well as *processes* of power, and needs to develop a critical perspective to what she/he learns *while* learning it.

Therefore ways have to be found of making visible to learners not steeped in them, the patterns and designs of written academic genres. This must include the process, as well as the product of the genre itself. In order to understand a ballet and how it is made, you have to go backstage and into the dressing rooms and watch the dancers limbering up in their legwarmers, rubbing resin into their shoes so that they don't slip, banging their pointe shoes violently on the floor to soften them so that they don't make a loud noise on stage. You need to see the corns and calluses on a dancer's feet and know the physical pain and exhaustion of their art. You need to see how their lipstick and false eyelashes are applied. You need to go to classes and watch the hours of work at the barre. Here you find the process, not just the product. Exposing students to the messy sides of academic discourse genres, letting them in on the process, as well as explicitly talking about the forms and functions of the genre, the role of a particular dance in a particular community, will help them to begin at least to understand the dance, though they may not choose to dance it.

Freedman and Medway (1994) sound a note of warning about the teaching of genres: when one teaches a certain genre, for example the genre of scientific report-writing, in a school, it becomes a new genre, that of writing science in the school, with a different purpose, function and audience. Similarly, the academic essay, whilst mimicking the genre of the research article, has a different function and audience. This does not mean it has no educational value; it does mean that the limits of explicit teaching of genres outside of the actual contexts where those genres occur need to be understood. Because genres are social forms intimately tied up with social processes, they remain a matter of intimate, local knowledge, with only incomplete access available to outsiders. One can teach break dancing in a dance studio, but it is only when it is danced on the street that it can be fully understood.

However, we can conceive of the genres of undergraduate academic writing, such as the report or the essay, as genres in their own right, which are not only mimicking the 'real' genres such as the research article or report. In so doing, we begin to ask questions about the educational role and specific functions of that particular genre. We are then able to teach its shape, its process and its functions more explicitly.

3

Plagiarism, 'originality' and copyright: *a striptease*

In this chapter I argue that the concept of plagiarism itself is constructed and relative, and is becoming increasingly problematic with new understandings of discourses and texts.

I shall discuss plagiarism and referencing from three perspectives. After looking at problems of definition of plagiarism, I turn to the first perspective, the development of the notion of plagiarism across time, from its earliest usage to the present. This will include a discussion of the history of copyright, which is intimately bound up with plagiarism. Alongside this I will discuss the concepts of 'autonomous text' and 'decontextualized' language, and attempt to show that these notions are problematic, and that language is intensely social, at the level of discourses, genres, and the word. The second angle is a snapshot of present-day writing genres, and how they deal with source documentation in different ways. My purpose in presenting the first two perspectives is to denaturalize the notion of plagiarism by relativizing it. It is also to put forward understandings of language which run counter to the grand narratives of 'originality' and 'autonomy' in writing. The third point of focus is the development of the student writer, on whom present-day genres of academic writing, and the historically constructed notions of plagiarism, converge. Here the discussion centres on the development of the undergraduate student as a writer, and some of the things that may be happening when a student is seen to be plagiarizing. I have divided these processes of development into six sections, though they may run parallel with one another, and they may interact with one another. These are the 'alienness' of academic discourses, the hybridization of discourses, the need to 'try on' academic discourses, the lack of authority of the student writer and her relationship to the authority of the sources, and the role that memory plays in the learning of language and of academic discourse. I look finally at what the meaning of authorship might be in an intensely social view of language, and at the complexity of developing authorial voice in writing.

Definitions of plagiarism: *Dance of the Seven Veils*

What is plagiarism? I gathered the following definitions of the word *plagiarize* from various dictionaries:

> *Webster's New World Dictionary*: to take (ideas, writings, etc.) from (another) and pass them off as one's own.

> *Oxford Advanced Learner's Dictionary of Current English*: take and use somebody else's ideas, words, etc. as if they were one's own.

> *Concise Oxford Dictionary*: 1. take and use (the thoughts, writings, inventions etc. of another person) as one's own. 2. pass off the thoughts etc. of another person as one's own. [L *plagiarus*, kidnapper]

> *Collins Dictionary of the English Language*: to appropriate (ideas, passages, etc.) from (another work or author). From Latin *plagiarus* plunderer, from *plagium* kidnapping.

The first two definitions, and the second Oxford definition, centre on the idea of plagiarism as *fraud*, as using the ideas of others *as if* they are one's own. The first definition of the *Concise Oxford Dictionary* modifies this slightly, saying 'take and use as one's own'. Here there is less sense of misrepresentation, simply of appropriation of ideas. These definitions seem to see plagiarism as possible in many forms: of thoughts, words, inventions. The *Collins* definition is quite different. The sense of intentional misrepresentation is much weaker, and, with the words *work* and *author*, it seems to be possible only in print of some kind.

Plagiarism is usually understood as 'intention to deceive', but, as the *Collins* definition shows, even this has come under dispute. The American Historical Association (AHA) has modified its definition of plagiarism, and taken out all references to 'intention to deceive' (Mooney, 1992). This is because scholars usually defend themselves from charges of plagiarism by saying that it was unintentional, and the new policy is an attempt to get scholars to take seriously the checking of their sources against their own writing. This, however, is an unusual understanding of plagiarism, arising out of a number of cases in which plagiarism was alleged but the AHA was unable to prove it.

So whether plagiarism relates only to print, or whether it also pertains, say, for oral speeches, or design ideas, is opaque. Whether it means intention to deceive, or simply appropriation of ideas and words without acknowledgement, is also disputed. The etymology of the word *is*, however, clear: the derivation from the Latin word meaning 'kidnap' or 'plunder' is indicative of how since its first usage in this way it has been regarded as a criminal activity

– parallel to stealing other people's offspring! Imitation is an important part of the learning process. Plagiarism 'criminalizes' imitation. This is why the concept needs unpacking.

The notion of authorship has been questioned by postmodern theorists such as Barthes, Derrida and Foucault (Bannet, 1989). In a world of rapid advances in communication technology, profound changes in the way we interact and communicate with each other are occurring, changes whose consequences for authorship are yet to be understood. Old laws of copyright are not adequate to deal with the exchanges of information possible on electronic networks, and global conference networking. The concept of plagiarism may have to undergo substantial transformation.

Scollon (1994) sees academic writing today as in the process of moving away from the old forms of attribution which served academic writing in modern times. He sees technological advances such as ERIC files of abstracts and references as making it possible for writers of academic discourse 'to get by without making any attempt to return to original sources' (43). Not only this, but because these files may be secondary or tertiary constructions (for example, an ERIC listing may contain an abstract reduced from an abstract from conference proceedings, of which only limited copies were printed) it may be difficult to locate the original. The sheer volume of writing available also makes getting through it in the original form an impossible task. He also perceives a current development towards a more oral and electronic system of referencing, through conference and e-mail chatting.

Another interesting problem which Scollon (1994) poses is that of the idea which gains so much currency that it is no longer referenced to its original source. He gives the example of Hymes' theory of communicative competence, which he says most students of today will most likely have come across in a publication later than 1972 when it was originally mentioned, and probably not in a publication by Hymes. He also makes the point that we do not mention the Enlightenment and then reference Kant. Failure to make such a reference is not counted as plagiarism. The dividing line between what is common knowledge, and what are ideas attributable to first sources is difficult to discern. Whilst perhaps not a problem for academics who know the field, this is a real difficulty which students encounter in much of the writing which I have looked at in researching plagiarism.

What plagiarism is, then, is by no means easily defined, and it is important to trace the origins of the concept in order to show how it has arisen, and why its definition, whilst always indistinct, is now, I believe, becoming even more so. Pennycook (1994) writes:

> authorship and intellectual property grew as concepts within European modernism, were not part of a premodern European world, and may not be part of a postmodern world.

(280)

'Originality' and copyright

The origins of 'originality' in written discourses; the development of copyright

I do not think that in dance the notion of originality has ever been as strong as it is in written literature and other forms of writing. Perhaps this is because forms of notation are a fairly recent development, and only used by large formal companies. The concept of plagiarism did not exist until the Enlightenment, and is bound up with notions of copyright. In this section I discuss the historical development of copyright in the West, and notions of 'Originality' and the Romantic author.

Scollon (1995) traces the origins of copyright to the thinking of Kant, in his book *Science of Right* published in 1788. Rogers (1982) traces its origins in England to the Copyright Act in 1710. Mallon (1989), whose book on plagiarism gives a thorough overview of the development of the concept, writes:

> Originality – not just innocence of plagiarism but the making of something really and truly new – set itself down as a cardinal literary virtue sometime in the middle of the eighteenth century and has never since gotten up.
>
> (24)

Before this time, and before the time of the commercial utilization of printed material, there was no sense of artistic 'ownership'. On the contrary, before the eighteenth century, one finds the text which displays its lineage through clearly identifiable, and sometimes unidentifiable, use of the texts of others, unacknowledged. The reader who is able to identify the uses and transformations of known texts enters into a bond of erudition with the author (Randall, 1991).

Renaissance literary practices: *folk dancing*

Folk dances have been largely unrecorded, and most people learn to do them by watching and imitating. They are passed down from generation to generation, partly preserved by repetition, but gradually changing over the years. Thomas (1994) discusses the Renaissance 'commonplace' book, which was a table book, often a gift to the owner, in which the owner was invited to write poetry and prose. These books consisted mainly of poems transcribed without attribution, and new compositions based on old by the owner. For instance, a poem based on another well-known poem, or on a psalm from the Bible, relies on the reader's recognition of previous poetry for its meaning. The original, the new and the commonplace book itself might contain no reference to authors. Reader and writer are combined in a compiler of old and new. As Thomas puts it,

The compiler acts ... not as ... a terminus; rather someone who channels the energies of poetic discourse and then reintroduces them into the cultural flow from whence they were written/read.

(415)

Feather (1994), however, argues that authors did have some rights as early as the sixteenth century in England, as they were sometimes paid for their works, but 'copyright' usually vested in the stationers, the trade guild to which members of the book trade belonged. At this time, however, 'copyright' basically meant a licence to print copies, and the power of the stationers' guild was closely tied to censorship and the Crown. According to Feather, the first glimmering of a notion of plagiarism was as early as 1584, where in the Stationers' Register a recipe book was registered, on the condition that it was not 'collected out of anie book already extante in printe in English' (Feather, 1994: 207). However, the notion of the author as creator of unique and original work, who could own words as literary property, only began in the Romantic period.

The Romantic notion of authorship: *Lord of the Dance*

In the Romantic period, there was a glorification of the individual and the authentic artistic imagination as a source of truth. The first time that an author went to court to defend his literary rights seems to have been in 1741, when Alexander Pope protested against the publication of correspondence between himself and Jonathan Swift (Rose, 1994). Pope wanted rights in Swift's letters to him, as well as in the letters that he himself had written. An important principle was established here, in that the court decided that copyright in a letter belongs to the writer, not the person who has the letter materially in his or her possession: essentially copyright was seen as immaterial, intellectual rather than physical property, from this moment onwards.

However, at the same time, notions of borrowing and sharing in a tradition of ideas and words coexisted, and still coexist, with the growth of copyright in law. Woodmansee (1994) documents the collaborative writing processes of Samuel Johnson. Johnson took freely from other works in his great collections, and also 'ghostwrote' many letters and lectures for friends, and exchanged sermons with other clerics. At the same time, Johnson 'helped to create the modern myth that genuine authorship consists in individual acts of origination' (Woodmansee, 1994: 21) both by opposing false attribution of authorship, and by publishing *Lives of the Poets* in which he established a collection of great authors whose work differed qualitatively from 'ordinary' literary labour. The Romantic notion of authorship is still with us today.

An interesting aspect of this Romantic notion of the author and its legal application today is that intellectual property has to be in some sense 'creative' or 'literary', and only then is it copyrightable. An American case, decided in 1991, which demonstrates this principle, is documented by the legal theorist Jaszi (1994). A telephone book company sued for copyright infringement when its alphabetical listings were copied and published by another firm. The court held that a telephone book, even when it is a compilation which has not existed before, is not sufficiently creative to be 'original'. So, interestingly, the labour and effort involved in putting together such a book is not recognized by the law, at least in the United States, as copyrightable. 'Plagiarizing' such a work is legal. It seems, then, that the notion of reward for the *labour* of writing has become secondary in present-day thinking about copyright; the principle of protection of livelihood for the author therefore seems less of a consideration than creative 'originality'.

Creative transformation and borrowing: *Excuse-me dancing*

Ever since the beginnings of ideas of copyright, there has been tension between protecting the rights of the author, and his or her means of livelihood, and allowing creative transformation of others' ideas and words to take place. Let us consider some of the creative transformations which take place today. In many forms of literature, particularly poetry, and in art and architecture, there are references (without acknowledgement) to previous famous works. Mellers (1982) uses music as an example of art which used to be 'common property', saying that composers such as Handel drew on the work of others as a 'common heritage' (414), transforming and enriching this heritage. He argues that 'originality became . . . the pearl that was certainly not without a price' (414). Borrowing in music has always been prevalent, but today technology has introduced a new form: the technique of electronic 'sampling' from previously recorded works. The ability to compile such a collage is a form of creativity, its result 'original'. Copyright law is struggling to keep up with such creative borrowings.

Harold Bloom (1982) maintains that 'good poems, novels and essays are webs of allusion, sometimes consciously and voluntarily so, but perhaps to a greater degree without design' (413). Bloom's only problem with 'plagiarism' seems to be that 'great writers only should be plagiarized. To copy second-rate authors indeed is immoral' (413). Sutherland (1982) laments the loss of communal artistic wealth, by saying that copyright has had a 'freezing effect', which resulted in Benjamin Walter's paradox, 'the novel marks the end of story-telling' (in Sutherland, 1982: 414). Ian McEwan (1982) acknowledges that writers borrow from each other, but it is when they are not aware of the source of influence that they are most likely to be accused of plagiarism: 'the more celebrated their source, the less likely they are to be accused of plagiarism. It is when they borrow without knowing it that they are most vulnerable to attack' (414). He also relates an instance in his own work where he ended a novel with an idea that he had unknowingly gleaned from a poem he had read a year before writing the scene. Only when he reread the poem did he remember the source of his idea. 'Is this plagiarism or a borrowing, or an "influence?"' he asks (414). Pat Rogers (1982) argues that absorption of the minds of others is what makes the truly creative mind, and puts it thus: 'You and I may lease the imaginative space of books. . . . It takes another creator to colonize that space' (414). T.S. Eliot, too, whose own work was full of allusions to the work of others, made the point that good poets make what they borrow into 'something better, or at least different' and that the more conscious the borrowing is, the more acceptable (in Mallon, 1989: 26).

An interesting case of conscious literary borrowing occurred in South Africa in 1995, when a high-ranking academic was accused of plagiarism. He had written a short story which used paragraphs, closely copied, from a Pulitzer-prize-winning novel, in an exercise of 'experimentation, adaptation and transformation' (Mzamane, in Garson, 1995: 8). He had deliberately omitted a dedication to the original author, 'saying that authors prefer to discover for themselves influences or literary references' (Garson, 1995: 8). Had he intended to be fraudulent, he would surely have been more subtle, and would have chosen a lesser-known work to plagiarize.

Randall (1991) discusses two cases of plagiarism which had deliberate, subversive intention, and the different ways in which they were received. The first book, *Trou de mémoire* by Hubert Aquin published in 1968, examines issues of identity and textual identity, and uses overt plagiarism – overt copying of another novel, as well as extensive copying from encyclopaedias (which was not seen as plagiarism). The book was lauded and received awards, its plagiarism benignly accepted as part of its power. The second book, *Le Devoir de violence*, written by the Malian novelist Yambo Ouologuem, uses a traditional African oral storytelling style, and was also highly acclaimed in Europe as the 'authentic' African novel, until critics discovered that sections had been plagiarized from Graham Greene's and André Schwarz-Bart's work. Greene filed suit and the work had to be republished with the offending sections cut out. The author's deliberately subversive strategy, intentionally borrowing from international works, and the way in which the book was received, drew attention to the fact that the West values the folkloric, the traditional in African art and literature, when in fact

> the real Africa is precisely the one that the West rejects in the form of accusations of plagiarism. Formed by Western values and cultures . . . modern African writers are as literate and as steeped in Western literature and cultural knowledge as are their Western counterparts.
>
> (Randall, 1991: 537)

I would like to pause here to consider the important aspect of intentionality in plagiarism. Generally it is accepted that unintentional copying is 'sloppy scholarship', which is usually condoned though at the same time disapproved of. It is where plagiarism is intentionally deceptive that it is most strongly condemned. The plagiarist deceives us by pretending that the work she/he is presenting is her/his own. This is intention to *deceive*. However, there is the other form of plagiarism, which I have reported above. This is conscious borrowing, but its intention is not to deceive, but to *plagiarize*. The intention is that the reader should recognize the plagiarism, discover the source; this is part of the literary game. Here, too, the thrill is in the hunt for the source, but the author expects and writes for exposure: the true plagiarist writes to conceal the source. The former practice is a highly risky strategy in today's world of tight copyright laws, but it is deliberately subversive of these, and this form of intertextuality, though increasingly supported by postmodern theory, is increasingly condemned by the law. Even parody, which mimics in order to critique, is becoming increasingly difficult under today's copyright laws.[1]

Another important distinction must be made in any discussion of plagiarism and copyright, which is that while plagiarism is generally considered to be the borrowing of other people's ideas and/or their words without acknowledgement, in copyright there is no protection of ideas, only the words used to express the ideas. There is an important reason for this: several people may have the same idea, especially when they are working with similar material, in a way which leads them to similar conclusions. Plagiarism of ideas is very difficult to prove. And yet it is included in the concept of plagiarism in academia so that students are made aware that ideas, too, can 'belong' to others, and their use should be acknowledged. However, in student writing, the monitoring of plagiarism in writing may prevent the marker of an assignment from allowing that a student may have come to their own conclusions, developed through their reading, which may be similar to those of another author, which, however, the student may not have read. Thesen (1997: 502) quotes a student in an interview who says the following:

> Sometimes you come up with what you feel is your personal feeling and then you're told that you're plagiarising some White guy who happened to be fortunate to get information and to jot it down, not because you're stealing his ideas. At times, you didn't even see the book, you are just analysing the situation, and then you put your facts and then you are told that, heh, this is not your point. You're plagiarising someone. And at times you don't feel free, you don't know who said it, and it really, limit, you know, it really limits us.

This kind of engagement with ideas, in order to reach one's own conclusions, is surely what we wish to encourage students to do. In Part II, I examine the negative consequences of monitoring of plagiarism in more detail, with reference to the students who participated in the research for this book.

So, generally, borrowing is a tradition in literature and other art forms and more than a tradition: creativity feeds on what has gone before, new work is formed out of old, but present-day copyright laws and the ethics of plagiarism effectively allow only borrowing with overt acknowledgement, a practice which the conventions of some genres of writing, such as the novel or short story, do not encourage.

Copyright protection has gone so far that where copyright exists, it is virtually impossible to draw on the copyrighted work as raw material for a new work. Plagiarism carries with it an enormous cost, ruining the careers of academic or literary figures, and causing the expulsion of students from their institutions. On the other hand, some traditional work, particularly in the Third World, receives no copyright protection, and can be exploited. Disney's appropriation of traditional folk tales such as *The Lion King* and *Pocahontas* is an example of how a major corporation now makes billions out of copyright for what were communal treasures (Lunsford and West, 1996). The challenge of copyright law, then, is to create a situation which encourages artistic creativity through just reward for creators of artistic work, while at the same time acknowledging that creativity feeds off what has gone before. The legal theorist Yen (1994: 159) goes so far as to say:

> Authorship is possible only when future authors have the ability to borrow from those who have created before them. If too much of each work is reserved as private property through copyright, future would-be authors will find it impossible to create.

Foucault (1984) adds an interesting observation to the historical progression of literature from something communally owned to something 'originated' and owned by an author. He too sees this progression in literature, but sees a reverse progression in science, where the truth value of scientific texts of the Middle Ages, on cosmology or medicines, say, was dependent on the authority of the author, such as Hippocrates or Pliny. He sees a reversal occurring in the seventeenth or eighteenth century, when

> Scientific discourses began to be received for themselves, in the anonymity of an established or always redemonstrable truth; their membership in a systematic ensemble, and not the reference to the individual who produced them, stood as their guarantee.

> (1984: 109)

This is an important point when considering the effect of the genre of a text on the conventions of referencing: the discourses of science, like the discourses of business, are more corporately owned, it seems, and collaboration is accepted as part of the process of making meaning. I would now like to consider how the (mythical) notion of the Romantic author, and the legal expression of this notion in copyright protection, comes into conflict with the realities of collaboration in writing processes.

Romantic authorship, copyright and collaboration:
it takes two to tango

Truly collaborative work, because of the author-centred notion inherent in copyright, cannot receive copyright protection. Jaszi (1994) argues that the law today cannot 'imagine' collaborative artistic processes, and has to 'reimagine' them 'so as to suppress complicating details about their modes of production' (38). With the tendency towards ever-increasing protection from imitation, there is a danger that what Jaszi calls 'serial collaborations' (40), i.e. works produced by elaborating on ideas or texts by many authors over years or generations, may be halted. In pre-literate Western culture and in literate and pre-literate cultures today, many oral art forms,[2] such as the oral poetry of the praise poets or *Imbongi* in South Africa, are essentially what Jaszi would call 'serial collaborations', in which poetry or narrative is remembered, embellished and transformed with each voicing. Often formulaic in order to aid recall and to allow the poet to 'improvise' upon the set rhythms and repetitions, as well as to aid reception and absorption by an audience, and intended to be ephemeral, something shifts fundamentally when these works are written down and copyrighted: the rights of new poets to the traditions of the poetry are blocked. There is an argument by music samplers that copyright in music is inherently Western European, in that it only recognizes melody and lyrics, and not rhythms (Sanjek, 1994). We could draw a parallel to literature here, in that copyright only recognizes written forms of text, and not oral texts, until these have been recorded and reproduced in print form. So 'serial collaborations' are a positive reality which copyright impacts upon.

Another reality is that much of writing is, in fact, collaborative in some way: the Romantic notion of the solitary author creating masterpieces on his/her own, is a fantasy: creativity thrives on interaction with others, ideas and words are born out of talk about ideas and about words. Similarly, many choreographed dance pieces are 'workshopped', using the ideas of the dancers, and (usually) bearing the name of the facilitating choreographer as the creator of the work, with acknowledgements to the dancers. Lunsford and Ede (1994) maintain that almost all writing in professional settings is done collaboratively and that 'the traditional model of solitary authorship is more myth than reality' (418). Much academic writing, too, is collaborative, whether it is in the form of joint authorship, whether it involves reporting on research done by a team, or whether it involves discussion around ideas before writing. I know that I have never written any academic article or report without a great deal of collaboration in some form with my colleagues and students, and my work is much the richer for their input and feedback.

Many educationists today try to incorporate group methodologies into their teaching, and in process-writing methodologies, which are widely practised at all levels of composition studies and writing pedagogy today, peer feedback on writing is incorporated as the minimal form of collaboration – very often texts are a joint construction of the group. Vygotskian theories, of how learning occurs through interaction with others, particularly with a more able peer or with an adult, have gained a great deal of currency in education in the last decades. However, just as copyright does not easily recognize collaboration, most methods of assessment, particularly the solitary examination situation, do not recognize collaborative work, but rather punish it where traces of collaboration are seen as plagiarism. Therefore, in its 'washback' effect, the reward/punishment system of the institution does not encourage what many see as optimal (collaborative) forms of learning. Lunsford and Ede call for the establishment of an 'ethics of collaboration' (1994: 438) rather than the pervasive obsession with the ethics of intellectual property ownership.

The power of collaboration is documented by Gere (1994), who describes the collaborative processes of sharing and writing texts in nineteenth-century women's clubs, when the clubs took communal ownership of both the texts they bought and the texts they wrote. They appropriated and rewrote the texts of their own members across generations, they wrote parodies of Biblical and classical texts, and always read their papers to other members (presumably for feedback leading to revision) before presenting them to the full group. Their writing subverted the ideologies of authorship and individual text ownership.

So copyright is not always and everywhere a 'good thing'. It places restrictions on collaborative processes and causes conflict within these. It alters and can restrict the development of some art forms. I have not even dealt with issues of copyright and 'fair use' – availability for those who cannot afford to buy copies. Suffice to say that copyright law is gradually tightening the noose around photocopying and recording practices, and the result is often that those who cannot afford to buy legitimate copies are denied access to that work. This must be of concern to teachers and especially academics: in situations of high student numbers, where the demands placed on library copies are impossibly great, penalties for photocopying are increasingly high, and many students simply cannot afford their own copies. Where once, in South African and UK universities, academics could compile photocopied course readers for students, this is now much more difficult – permission for the use of each reading has to be obtained from the publishers, with the result that readings may be chosen depending on ease of obtaining permission rather than on quality. Access is generally being restricted, and this has implications for educators and students. Again, a balance has to be found between just rewards and access: indiscriminate and widespread photocopying practices are destructive to the production of knowledge and literature, but equally destructive are copyright laws and plagiarism practices which tightly circumscribe interactive and collaborative practices, thereby curtailing creativity, and limiting access to information. Lunsford and West (1996) pose the question 'who gains if the public commons loses? . . . whose interests are being served by the current intellectual property regime?' (389). They find that it is not the author who benefits so much from copyright, but large commercial companies. I think copyright does provide important protection for authors, but obsessive policing of it is counter-productive. Similarly, awareness of plagiarism and citation conventions can help students to develop their own voices, whilst obsessive monitoring of this can be destructive. Copyright and its ethical counterpart, plagiarism, have not always been with us, and in some art forms and genres of writing today, they are not, and should not be, a major issue. The second perspective, that I shall deal with in the next chapter, looking at plagiarism through the lens of different genres of writing, will demonstrate this. Before moving on to this, however, I would now like to turn to a concept which runs parallel to that of 'originality', the concept of the autonomous text.

'Autonomous' text, context and intertextuality: *the soloist and the corps*

Notions of 'autonomous text' and 'decontextualized' language are to be found in many educational constructions of what the written academic text should try to achieve. Theorists such as Cummins and Swain (1986) have been highly influential, certainly in the Academic Development field in South Africa, in trying to account for the apparent gap between bilingual students' oral proficiency in their second language and their academic achievement when studying in their second language. In their interpretation of the interrelationship between language proficiency and academic achievement, academic language is seen as 'context reduced', meaning that 'shared reality cannot be assumed, and thus linguistic messages must be elaborated precisely and explicitly so that the risk of misinterpretation is minimized' (1986: 153). They give the example of writing or reading an academic article as being one of the most 'context-reduced communicative behaviours' and therefore the most difficult for a speaker of another language. Cognitive Academic Language Proficiency (CALP) is a cognitive functioning needed for success in school whilst BICS (Basic Interpersonal Communicative Skill) is a social functioning not as valuable for school success. In reading theory, it has been clearly demonstrated that the better the reader, the more extralinguistic context is being used in reading, such as prior information, knowledge of the discourse, and knowledge of the writer's context (Edelsky, 1991). The same holds true for writing. The notion of academic writing being 'context-reduced' is not a useful one; it seems rather that the difficulty of academic language lies more in its very *embeddedness* in a context, and the lack of embeddedness of the novice writer. Much of the meaning of the intricate hand movements or *mudras* in classical Indian dance is lost to the observer who is outside its context. To aim at writing a text that stands alone has little meaning: a text can only mean within a context. The notion of *explicitness* in writing, however, is still a useful educational concept.

Geisler (1994) traces the historical development of the ideal of the text that stands alone, culminating in Olson's 1977 coinage of the term 'autonomous text', which signified that in such a text, the meaning was perfectly explicit in the text itself, without reference to any other text, whether oral or written. Cazden (1992), in an essay entitled 'The Myth of Autonomous Text', argues strongly against this understanding of autonomous text. She maintains that nothing is explicit in writing, unless it relates and refers to what is known about a particular audience, though this knowledge is unwritten and unspoken. She further develops her argument by discussing the notion of intertextuality, which is inherent in all writing and so the notion of autonomous text is simply incorrect. She concedes that written texts are decontextualized, in that the contextual clues available to those communicating directly with each other, which would be present in an oral communication, are absent. But she sees the written text as 'massively contextualized with respect to contexts in the mind – contextualized first in the mind of the writer, and then recontextualized in the minds of readers' (148).

Recontextualization also means transformation. Fairclough (1992) writes of 'intertextual chains' in which texts are transformed when they are incorporated into, and become, part of other texts. A traditional African dance becomes another text altogether when performed on the mines as a tourist attraction. Or the advert for a watch which shows a dancer executing a 'precision movement', her legs at six o' clock. And so also the ways in which people use sources in writing transform those sources, give them new meanings.

One rationale often cited for meticulous source documentation is that the reader can return to the source and 'verify' the author's use of the source. This is what Spack (1997) does with respect to the sources used by Carson (in Spack, 1997) and the way in which Carson's work is subsequently used by other scholars. Spack criticizes Carson's 'selective scholarship' (771) because Carson presents only what is useful in her sources to her argument, so giving an unbalanced viewpoint. It must be said that recontextualization inevitably alters 'original' meaning. I have no doubt that the book you are reading now will be quoted to support arguments with which I would not be in agreement, and taken in directions which I have not conceived of: this is in the nature of recontextualization. All scholarship, I would contend, is inevitably selective and transformative of earlier research, with a fine line between distortion and legitimate interpretation.

Originality and autonomy as values are based on an ideology which tends towards individualism and competition, rather than community and cooperation, independence rather than interdependence, analysis rather than synthesis, commodification rather than intrinsic value. Referencing one's sources in academic writing, however, may be seen as running counter to individualistic values: it is both a form of access to verification, and a sharing of resources with readers. For instance, the fact that Carson had referenced her work enabled Spack to find her sources and read the full articles in question, so as to obtain a broader view. The 'sharing of resources' rationale for referencing makes sense to students, rather than one which emphasizes paying one's debts and avoiding theft of others' property.

Part of Cazden's 'massive contextualization' of text lies at the level of the genre, part of it at the level of the word. I shall first deal with the word, in particular with Bakhtin's view of the social nature of the meanings of words.

The social nature of language: *steps danced by many feet*

Bakhtin's work gives us the sense of language which teems with those who speak it, who have spoken it, and those who will hear or speak it. For Bakhtin, words are alive, alive with meanings and voices and dialogues, language is crowded with the meanings of the past, the present and the future. The voices which social languages contain serve as the rich source of creativity for the writer's own voice, without them, his 'prose nuances . . . do not sound' (1981: 278). The word is internally dialogic: it is shaped by the 'already uttered', other 'alien' words, and by the answer which it anticipates. In other words, the responses which are anticipated actually shape the meaning of the word, either resisting or supporting its sense, and 'enriching the discourse'. Thus, even at the level of the word, language is richly social. He writes:

> As a result of the work done by all these stratifying forces in language, there are no 'neutral' words and forms – words and forms that can belong to 'no one'; language has been completely taken over, shot through with intentions and accents. . . . All words have the 'taste' of a profession, a genre, a tendency, a party, a particular work, a particular person, a generation, an age group, the day and hour. Each word tastes of the context and contexts in which it has lived its socially charged life; all words and forms are populated by intentions. Contextual overtones (generic, tendentious, individualistic) are inevitable in the word.
>
> (1981: 293)

The question, for reflecting on plagiarism and copyright, which flows out of this intensely social view of language, is one of 'who owns meaning?', asked by Holquist (1981, in Wertsch, 1991). The response to this ranges from the view of individual authors or speakers creating their own meaning out of a neutral system of language, a viewpoint which would concur with the 'cultural ideal' of 'autonomous' text, to the response which Kress has, which is simply that 'no writers have their own words' (1985: 45). Perhaps no writers have their own words, but they have particular ways of working with those words which are their own. At this point I shall do a soft shoe shuffle from the dance metaphor, into another: I like Holquist's (in Wertsch, 1991: 68) metaphor of 'renting' meaning, where words are borrowed from and given back to the community, and sound within the voices of that community.

For the new student, newly entering the academic discourses, and having to start using the discourses in assignments, there is no other way than to be a squatter, to live in the discourses of academia without owning them, maybe using a student loan to be paid off at a later stage, or maybe not paying the rent at all, as at this stage she/he will not know how to give meaning back to the community. Giving back may come, but renting at this stage is essential. We all rent meaning: those of us who know the community well, know where and how to pay the rent. Some of us may come from a culture of non-payment to those who have colonized academic discourse, may feel uncomfortable in the landlord's spaces, and may choose never to pay the rent.

Having explored the social nature of the word, I now turn to genre, which is by definition a social concept, and examine how different genres deal with documentation and referencing, and what plagiarism means in different contexts.

Notes

1. For a discussion of recent legal decisions in the USA regarding parody in music, see Woodmansee and Jaszi, 1995.
2. Ong (1982) calls the term oral literature 'preposterous' (11), preferring 'oral art form', as such a self-contradictory term only indicates our difficulty in literate society in imagining pre-literate art forms.

4

Plagiarism and referencing across genres: *different moves to different tunes*

In this chapter I consider plagiarism from the second angle, a wide-angle shot of documentation across different genres, in order to demonstrate how the concept shifts depending on the writing context.

Using a genre approach, Jameson (1993) provides important insights into what constitutes plagiarism in different textual genres. She takes different genres, such as the novel, the news article, speeches and the business report, and shows how variable the notion of plagiarism is across these contexts, writing that 'what would constitute culpable plagiarism in one context might constitute proper use of sources in another context depending on the group whose expectations defined "misappropriation"' (20). I shall use her examples at some length, because I think they are instructive.

She describes, for instance, the process of a consulting firm doing an assignment for a client. Using multiple sources, including a nameless 'boilerplate' written ten years before, lifting extensive passages from previous filed reports, adding their own ideas, they write a report which involves the work of at least twenty people, and no author is credited. The work belongs to the corporation. Similarly, the annual report of the Academic Development Programme at the University of Cape Town is written by many individuals – there is a set of questions which goes out to all staff members, each centre or group of academics running a course collaboratively writes its own report, and this gets summarized and incorporated into one report compiled mainly by support staff, though the assumption may be that the directorate has authored it. It is modelled on and takes substantial sections from previous reports, and nobody gets credited.

The genre of the newspaper article involves different forms of documentation. Although plagiarism may be alleged if there has been word-for-word copying from unacknowledged sources, generally the genre 'neither requires nor permits citations, endnotes, bibliographies, or other textual indicators' (Jameson, 1993: 23). The speech, too, does not give much opportunity for acknowledgement, and it is not normally expected. A speech ghostwriter never needs to be credited, although she or he may be the real 'originator' of the actual speech. The very word 'ghostwriter' signals the invisibility of the real author.

The novel is also interesting in that, again, there is no way of crediting a source within a novel, other than with a dedication or a footnote. The genre does not permit it. As Jameson puts it: 'Novels as a genre do not include word-for word or closely paraphrased passages from other works. Such passages must simply be eliminated; they cannot be documented' (23). She points out that although historical information may be used in a novel, which obviously comes from somewhere, it does not need to be documented, whereas in an academic history it would need to be.

Another interesting insight from Jameson comes in her observation that even within academia, and within a discipline, genres differ regarding sourcing: the academic textbook needs to be in the author's own words, but it does not usually need to be documented with the same thoroughness that a scholarly journal article might require. It is my own observation that the amount and kind of documentation required differs widely across journals in my own field. A glance at the average article from the *TESOL (Teaching of English to Speakers of Other Languages) Quarterly* (many references) and that from the *English Language Teaching (ELT) Journal* (sometimes virtually no references) will confirm this. I was asked to write a short article about plagiarism in a local Applied Linguistics association newsletter. The editor required me to take almost all citations out of the article. The genre of the newsletter article does not have the stringent requirements of documentation of sources that an academic book has. The editors of the publication which you are reading, similarly wanted a pruning of academic references in rewrites of this book, taking it from thesis to book.

'Fact-based' fields such as medicine often use definitive manuals or textbooks which practitioners draw on to make their diagnoses. McCarthy (1991) explores the influence of a single text on the diagnostic processes and texts of a child psychiatrist, and concludes that her thinking and writing is highly structured by a particular text, known as DSM-III (Diagnostic and Statistical Manual of Mental Disorders). This manual was developed in the 1970s to standardize definitions of psychiatric disorders, facilitate communication regarding these, and enable correct prescription of medication. McCarthy finds that the manual defines the psychiatrist's interview schedule with the patient's family, what the psychiatrist considers relevant information for her diagnosis, as well as how she analyses that information, writes her diagnosis and decides on treatment. The psychiatrist refers directly to the DSM-III in writing up her clinical diagnosis, and the document is well known to her audience of medical practitioners working with her patients. Such a document, which McCarthy calls a 'charter document', holds enormous power to shape the work of a profession. However there is clearly no single author of this document (in fact it was written by a 130-member group) and copyright belongs to the American Psychiatric Association: the Romantic notion of the 'original author' cannot apply. There is no thought of 'plagiarism' in copying word-for-word indicators for diagnosis, for example, and no quotation marks are necessary. Citing a particular section number of the manual is more for ease of reference to a common document to which all practitioners will have access, than an expression of indebtedness to this text for ideas or information. Again this is an example of knowledge more corporately owned and shared, which seems to be more prevalent in the sciences. The assumption seems to be that 'facts' do not 'belong' to anybody, while ideas and words do. Once new research becomes incorporated into a body of knowledge, those who discovered these facts may be honoured by, for example, the naming of a disease after them, but the texts with which practitioners work in their everyday lives use the knowledge freely without attribution.

Devitt (1991) reports on fascinating research on intertextuality in the field of tax accountancy. She shows how text-based the profession is, like psychiatry, relying on a fairly small set of authoritative tax publications (such as Tax Court decisions or tax legislation). Such texts are continually quoted and referred to in all memos and correspondence that tax professionals use. Very often the exact section of an authoritative text is referred to in brackets, for example IRC sect 923 (3) (c), and sometimes its content is paraphrased, but mostly it is quoted word for word, to maintain accuracy. This word-for-word quotation is unmarked by quotation marks. Writing of interviews with tax accountants, Devitt says,

> Although some of the experts seemed self-conscious about the potential 'plagiarism' and several seemed unaware that they used unmarked quotation, most easily argued their rhetorical need for unmarked quotation. While choosing quotation for accuracy ... the writers often responded to the rhetorical situation of a lay audience by leaving the quotation unmarked.
>
> (349)

In other words, the accountant believes that the lay audience prefers what they think is the accountant's interpretation of the tax publication, but the accountant prefers the accuracy of the original text itself, so the quotation is left unmarked.

Genre-based research such as Devitt's has great potential for bringing to light such intricate social functions of referencing or 'plagiarizing'. Such research also points to the gap between the academy and the workplace: of what value are the genres of academic writing beyond the academy? It is clear from the above discussion, that kinds of documentation vary from genre to genre, but nowhere are the requirements for thorough documentation more stringent than in the genres of academic writing, although these differ across disciplines. In the light of the very different writing demands in the workplace, and thinking about the university as an educational institution, we need to think carefully about a writing pedagogy that seems to cater mainly to the small percentage of students who will continue to postgraduate work. Thinking about the university in terms of production of knowledge, it is clear that it requires its own genres and has its own very valid functions. We need to think about why we have these stringent requirements in academic writing, why these genres have developed in this way, what the role of referencing is in academic writing, both in knowledge production terms and in educational terms. Once we have clarified this for ourselves, we will be in a better position to make it explicit to our students. I shall return to the role and functions of referencing in academic writing in Chapters 8 and 12.

5

The development of the student writer: *from mimic to master*

In this chapter I turn to the third angle from which I view plagiarism and referencing, which focuses on the development of the student writer, and in particular how referencing and plagiarism relate to that development. The problems that I want to discuss here may occur at all stages of writing development, and interact with one another, i.e. they are not ordered stages of development. However, I have divided them into different sections, which discuss the stage when academic discourse is 'alien', the stage of 'trying on' academic discourse, the problem of hybridization of different discourses, the problem of illegitimate and legitimate language and how that plays itself out in undergraduate writing, the role of the learning of chunks of language in second-language acquisition, and the very complex process of developing authorial voice in writing.

Alien words: *dancing upon nothing*

When a dancer is learning a new routine, and new steps, there is a stage at which performing those steps means getting methodically from one step to the next. She cannot put her self into it, she has to think too hard about what comes next. She is dependent on copying the instructor or those dancing beside her. The dance feels outside of her, alien. All her energy goes into learning and just remembering what to do next. After a while the steps become more automatic, she begins to feel in control, and she may begin to feel confident enough to put in her own variations – she begins to relax and to really dance.

Beginning to 'own' the words, appropriating them for one's own purposes, is a difficult process. For some, words resist being owned and made anew, they 'sound foreign in the mouth of the one who has appropriated them and now speaks them' (Bakhtin, 1981: 294). This is an apt description, to me, of the struggles of new writers of academic discourse. Bakhtin continues:

[the words] cannot be assimilated into his context and fall out of it; it is as if they put themselves in quotation marks against the will of the speaker. Language is not a neutral medium that passes freely and easily into the private property of the speaker's intentions; it is populated – overpopulated – with the intentions of others. Expropriating it, forcing it to submit to one's own intentions and accents, is a difficult and complicated process.

(1981: 294)

The inarticulateness of the novice writer is not surprising when she/he is required to write using a 'foreign language' which is not yet owned by the student: the response may be simply to use the words of others, to ventri-loquize, but without a speaking voice, without modification. Wertsch (1991) sees Bakhtinian ventriloquism, i.e. 'the process whereby one voice speaks through another voice or voice type in a social language' (Wertsch, 1991: 59), as *'one of the fundamental processes of development'* (1991: 127, my italics). The key is, however, for the speaking, authorial voice to truly speak, albeit through the voices of others. This is what is so difficult for the novice writer of academic discourse (or for any writer) – it is the control of the voices so that the authorial voice speaks through them, it is 'forcing' language to 'sub-mit to one's own intentions and accents' which is the fundamental struggle of writing. When the student's own voice is not present, as it may not be if the student is conceptually and socially far removed from the discourse, the result is 'voiceless' writing, where the writer's alienation is so profound that the voices of the sources used are not animated by the authorial voice. The dance is soulless and stilted.

This stage of alienation from academic discourse is beautifully described by a native Alaskan student, Martha Demientieff, in Cazden (1992). Begin-ning an assignment for a course on classroom discourse, she writes:

As I began work on this assignment, I thought of the name of the course and thought I had to use the word 'discourse'. The word felt like an intruder in my mind displacing my word 'talk'. I could not organize my thoughts around it. It was like a pebble thrown into a still pond disturbing the smooth water. It makes all the other words in my mind out of sync. When I realized that I was using too much time agonizing over how to write the paper, I sat down and tried to analyze my problem. I realized that in time I will own the word and feel comfortable using it, but until that time my own words were legitimate. Contrary to some views that exposure to the dominant culture gives one an advantage in learning, in my opinion it is the ownership of words that gives one confidence. I must want the word, enjoy the word and use the word to own it. When the new word becomes synonymous in my head as well as externally, then I can think with it.

(In Cazden, 1992: 190)

The realization that Demientieff has, that her own words are 'legitimate' until such time as she truly 'owns' the words of the academic discourse, is one that not all students come to. If you know that 'discourse' can mean 'talk', you are already on your way to 'owning' the word, because it is beginning to connect to your own semantic landscape, though it may put it 'out of sync'. New students may struggle to make any connections at all, and that is when they are unable to use their own words, because their conceptual and social distance from the discourse is too profound; the shoes are vacant.

'Trying on' the discourse: *stepping into the shoes*

I imagine that Demientieff's next stage will be to try out the word 'discourse' one day, to see how it feels and fits. The new student has to put on those dancing shoes, and they may feel very silly at first. The only beginning he or she may feel able to make, is to copy very closely and deliberately the movements of another. It may look like plagiarism.

Writing of a particular at-risk nursing student whose writing was a patchwork of copied bits of text, Hull and Rose (1990) put forward the notion that it is important for the student to 'try on' the discourse of a profession or an academic discourse, in order to eventually 'own' the discourse fully. For this particular student, the words were 'alien' in the way that Bakhtin describes, and the only way she could try to make them her own was to imitate them with a few changes. Not only was she 'trying on' another language, in this way, but also another persona. They write that

> A fundamental social and psychological reality about discourse, oral or written, is that human beings continually appropriate each other's language to establish group membership, to grow, and to define themselves in new ways.
>
> (1990: 242)

Appropriation can take place in the form of words, themes, topics, registers and discourses, and the appropriation may be more or less successful in its new form. My own son, Raymond, as a small boy, read a delightful story poem called *Tim Kipper*, in which Tim, who is a smoker, grows a chimney on his head from all his smoking. Eventually he can no longer hide it under top hats or dustbins, and he has to go to hospital to have it cut off and to stop smoking. About two years later, concerned about his grandmother's smoking, Raymond wrote and sent her a story in which she grew a chimney on her head. The theme was basically the same, the main character was different, and the form (prose narrative instead of rhyme) was also new. He had stored the story in his memory, and appropriated much of the content, but adapted it to suit the new purpose: trying to get Granny to stop smoking! Lensmire and Beals (1994) studied a similar process of appropriation and adaptation in children's writing. They examine how Suzanne, writing a book, appropriated much of her material from a novel she had read, in addition to adapting well-known rhymes. She also used names, social events and relations and current colloquialisms from her peer group. Some of these were conscious appropriations, some unconscious. In appropriating aspects of a novel she had read, she was 'trying on' the discourse of a novel: I would suggest that this was part of her development as a writer, on her way to finding her own voice. Using the voices of others successfully in one's own writing means making one's own voice speak through the voices of others. I return to this later.

'Trying on' academic discourse is one way of understanding plagiarism when considering a student's entry into academic discourse. This could take the form of appropriation of the lexis of the new discourse, of the structure of the academic essay, for example, or it could be in the form of whole phrases or sentences in a mosaic which barely contains a sense of the student as author.

Hybridization of discourses: *toyi-toyis and tutus*

International media reportage of South Africa in the 1980s and early 1990s abounded with images of angry protesters doing the toyi-toyi, a war dance which was appropriated into the political events of the time. Many white students were amongst those protesting against the injustices of apartheid, and many were compelled to try to do the toyi-toyi. It didn't always look quite right. The toyi-toyiers who knew how, moved their backs and shoulders with wonderful looseness and flexibility. Those who were learning kept their backs and torsos very stiff and all the movement was in the legs and arms. They were often self-conscious, uncomfortable and awkward, and this also hindered their movement. The classically trained ballet dancer might have even more difficulty in loosening up that back – years of training have taught her to hold it stiff, shoulders down, butt tight. I would like to use Bakhtin's concept of hybridization to explain the mixing of new and old discourses, and how this may result in 'plagiarism', to discuss another stage of development in a student's writing. This may run parallel to the 'alienation' and 'trying on' stages.

Bakhtin's term 'hybridization' means 'the mixture of two social languages within the limits of a single utterance' (1981: 358). He uses this notion to unravel the different 'social languages' (close to what Gee means by discourse) used by a writer in any text. These may be unconscious or intentional. 'Social languages', or discourses, interpenetrate and mingle; Bakhtin seems to see them as doing battle with one another.

Similarly, for Kress (1985), discourses are not monolithic and impenetrable, they exist not in isolation but sometimes in opposition to or different from many other discourses, and they are dynamic and shifting. Kress believes that where some discourses are more powerful than others, they act as 'colonizers', tending to flatten and harmonize differences and discontinuities by 'making that which is social seem natural and that which is problematic seem obvious' (1985: 11). The individual carries traces of past and present discourses, indicative of the social positions that individual has taken up. In academic writing, then, traces of these different discourses may be manifested in a student's writing, until a 'harmonizing' of these differences take place, and academic writing becomes as 'natural' as it is to the lecturer steeped in the practice of his or her discipline. The torso loosens up. White Men *Can Dance*.

In Angélil-Carter and Thesen (1993), Thesen uses biographical sketches and analyses of student writing to uncover 'different literacy practices' (20).[1] She demonstrates how traces of students' other literacy practices, such as informal, oral discourse, the discourse of the political organization, and Biblical discourse intermingle, 'cut across' and conflict with the academic discourse that they are learning in English for Academic Purposes (EAP) (19). These mixings of literacies within academic writing are forms of unintentional hybridization. When we get a new student learning how to write in a discipline, therefore, what may manifest itself in their writing is the unsuccessful, conflictual hybridization of prior school (or other) discourses and new academic ones.

Such hybrids should not always be seen as negative and conflictual, but may facilitate a smooth transition into academic writing. An example of prior discourses both facilitating and hindering a student writer is found in Clark and Ivanic (1997). They examine a philosophy essay on environmental ethics written by a mature student, Sarah. They posit six different 'identities' which Sarah draws on in her writing, for example, 'identity as an insider to the nuclear industry', 'identity as a natural scientist', 'identity as a member of the academic community'. All of these are identifiable in the actual writing. They point out that as Sarah's life history included the death of her husband through leukaemia while he was working at an atomic energy institute, it was very difficult for her to approach her assignment 'objectively'. However, many of Sarah's life experiences enabled her to argue her case more effectively. Thus Sarah's 'identities' enabled her to draw on past discourses, some of which conflicted with the essay she was writing, but some of which supported it.

The losses suffered in smoothing out hybridized writing, in creating seamless uniform textures, should be recognized. The 'harmonizing' that Kress (1985) speaks of is problematic, not necessarily a desirable goal. Harmony may mean colonization, as Kress indicates, and results in losses for both colonizer and colonized. In an interesting ethnographic study, Chiseri-Strater

(1991) followed closely the 'public and private discourse' of two students (one male and one female), examining the interaction of the public (within the university institution) and the private discourses. She concludes that the curricula of the academy do not successfully utilize the rich potential of the private literacies of these students, and also shows how female students are denied access to the discourses of some disciplines, which she sees as patriarchal and not valuing feminine ways of being. Here it seems that the private discourses are not permitted to enter the academy, and only interfere in problematic ways; the enriching potential is lost.

What could plagiarism mean in the context of hybridization? Moder and Halleck (1995) explore cultural differences in attitudes to the text, writing that in cultures 'founded on Confucian values, memorization and imitation are the mark of an educated person' (16). Memorizing and copying classical texts is the way that children in the People's Republic of China learn to write. Scholars also quote these texts verbatim because educated people will recognize the quote, and there is no need to cite sources. Respect for the text means faithful imitation, rather than presuming to write it differently from the original. Pennycook (1996) begins a discussion of plagiarism with reflection on his Chinese student who produced an essay on Abraham Lincoln, which had been memorized word for word from a high school textbook. The student, when asked about this text, had considered himself fortunate at being asked to write a biography of a famous person, because he had one memorized by heart! He had seen no problem with this strategy. When students accustomed to discourses such as these enter Western academic institutions, quoting the sages from memory is seen as plagiarism.

The point here is not to situate students in different cultural boxes in which they are held captive, or to 'excuse' them from plagiarism practices. It is rather to heighten awareness of prior, conflicting discourses, from which students can move. It is important, too, not to fall into the trap of assuming that because there is a tradition of memorization of text in China, this is the only tradition there is. Bloch and Chi (1995) completed a comparative study of the use of citations in academic writing in English and Chinese. They analysed 60 articles in each language from prestigious journals in different disciplines, and found, contrary to popular belief, that the Chinese writers of social science articles often did criticize previous research conclusions, but diplomatically, using different conventions, without naming any sources. They also made more frequent use of older texts, and less frequent use of new ones, indicating a veneration of classical texts as well as problems of access to newer texts. In science articles, however, the referencing conventions seemed to be very similar to Western conventions, possibly due to stronger Western influences on the field of science. They point out that Chinese rhetoric 'is not monolithic but . . . there are contending strands that have existed since Confucius' (270). They also discuss the influence of the Civil Service Exams, a powerful system of examinations which had to be passed in order for anybody to obtain coveted government jobs. Knowledge of the Confucian classics was necessary for obtaining any government post. Literacy practices were strongly shaped by these examinations, with an emphasis on memorization and the use of a highly structured essay genre. The main thrust of their article is to bring a sense of complexity to Chinese rhetoric, as it is often seen as coherent and uniform. Whilst warning against any simplistic notions about Chinese rhetoric, Bloch and Chi however make it clear that many of the difficulties Chinese students have when writing in English in a Western institution, such as over-reliance on source texts and plagiarism, are consistent with some of their rhetorical traditions.

In the South African higher education context, the student who is plagiarizing may simply be making use of the modes of textual construction which she or he knew at school, which usually meant copying or at best closely paraphrasing an authoritative textbook. (See Appendix 1 for an analysis of students' prior writing experiences, and Chapter 10 for a discussion of this.) He or she is mixing this with an attempt at academic writing by sprinkling references throughout the text. Not only the prior mode of textual construction comes into play here, but also the previous understanding of the nature of knowledge, which is likely to be that knowledge is a set of facts out there to be learned. To be asked to synthesize, or compare and contrast different readings, to construct an argument in relation to texts, makes little sense when you understand that what you read is fact. Who wrote what is of little importance when all of it is the truth. Atkinson (1997) sees critical thinking as a social practice (*'critical thinking is cultural thinking'* is his summary of his argument, 89) and cites feminist critique of critical thinking as a distancing rather than a connecting practice. He surveys evidence that in non-Western, group-orientated cultures, respecting the group and its inheritance is socialized into children from an early age, and critical stances are difficult for students from these cultures. He does not seem to recognize, however, that though the social practices students bring with them into the institution may conflict with the positions they are being asked to take, students are rooted in, but not trapped by their prior literacy practices, and if shown explicitly how the new practice differs with the old, can begin to write using the (critical) practices of the new discourse.

An interesting example of plagiarism which may be explained in terms of hybridization is the famous case of Martin Luther King. Miller (1993) uses King's story to exhort his readers to reconsider the definitions of plagiarism. Not only did King plagiarize in his doctoral dissertation, and other graduate essays, but also in many of his famous speeches he used the words of others, unacknowledged. King, as a preacher and as an African American, was the bearer of a 'highly oral religious culture that treated songs and sermons as shared wealth, not private property' (A60). Miller sees his plagiarism in his academic work as a difficulty in 'negotiating the boundaries between oral and print traditions' (1993: A60).

Hybridization of discourses is one explanation, therefore, of what the 'plagiarizing' student may be doing. Bakhtin's notion of authoritative discourses, which will be elaborated in the section below, is important here too: the old authoritative discourses of the school, or of the church or mosque, of those other 'fathers', have to be discarded, the old costumes cleared out, and in that ongoing process strange hybrids may occur. Ballet dancers studying contemporary dance bring with them much that they can use, supple leg extensions, wonderful muscle control. But they do not know how to relax the body, to use the body's weight and momentum to move. They have much to learn and unlearn, much to discard and much to retain.

Illegitimate and legitimate language: *the masquerade*

Bourdieu[2] (1991), building on Austin's theory of speech acts, has a concept of 'legitimate' or 'authorized' language. He asserts that you do not find power within the actual linguistic manifestations of a speech act: power comes from outside. He writes:

> By trying to understand the power of linguistic manifestations linguistically, by looking in language for the principle underlying the logic and effectiveness of the language of institution, one forgets that authority comes to language from outside, a fact concretely exemplified by the skeptron that, in Homer, is passed to the orator who is about to speak. Language at most represents this authority, manifests and symbolizes it.
>
> (1991: 109)

Bourdieu understands that the power to speak is granted, it comes from outside, and it is not granted to all. A communicative event only takes place when the speaker is *recognized* as a legitimate speaker, and is not an 'impostor'. He has to be holding the 'skeptron'. This recognition and authority is granted under the conditions which 'define legitimate usage', one of which is: 'an utterance must be spoken by the person legitimately authorized to do so' (1991: 113).

The white toyi-toyiers, dancing what is essentially a war dance, did not always seem legitimate. Novice writers of academic discourse are not yet 'legitimate', they are 'impostors' in the sense that they are often required to write within what seems to be the genre of the research or journal article, and yet they have no real authority, and their audience is their tutor, and not a community of political scientists. Bartholomae (1985: 134) writes of students having to 'invent the university' every time they write, in that students are expected to write in the discourses of the disciplines before they are legitimate speakers of the language of the discipline. The result is that they invariably simply have to imitate the discourses of the disciplines until such time as they have actually learned to write them, until such time as they are no longer 'impostors', and are no longer 'inventing'. As Bartholomae puts it:

> [The student] . . . has to invent the university by assembling and mimicking its language while finding some compromise between idiosyncrasy, a personal history, on the one hand, and the requirements of convention, the history of a discipline, on the other. He must learn to speak our language. Or he must dare to speak it or to carry off the bluff, since speaking and writing will most certainly be required long before the skill is 'learned'.
>
> (1985: 134)

One of the masks which is part of 'our language' that the student has to don is that of disinterested displayer of factual knowledge. Swales (1990) carefully reconstructs the process whereby the art of scientific discourse developed into one where the reader is deceived into believing that there are no rhetorical devices, and that the author is presenting facts which speak for themselves. But of course it is all about rhetoric, and careful construction of argumentation. The disguise of the author behind this 'voiceless' factual construction (as manifested in the distaste for the personal pronoun 'I' in much academic discourse) is not easy: from a background of mainly expressive writing in English at school, and little writing in other subjects, the student launches into writing which is truly voiceless in an attempt at imitating a neutral stance. The result is that the stance of the writer to the 'facts' presented is not discernible, and there is no authorial presence animating the words.

Womack (1993) thoughtfully reflects on the development of the academic essay, uncovering similar ambivalences and pretences inherent in this form of writing. He argues that the essay is historically the 'literary sign of functional innocence' (46), which when used for assessment forces the student to adopt a role of 'free disinterestedness' in a highly functional competitive context. Another contradiction is the expectation of the production of independent thinking together with the demand that all assertions be supported by evidence, and that arguments must be balanced. To use Womack's words: 'in short, that the expression of independence of mind be thoroughly permeated by signs of conformity to an academic code of practice' (46). For Womack, plagiarism is 'the inevitable stress signal of this tension' (46), where the pretence induced by the genre shifts minutely to the pretence of literally adopting the words of others, not only a role. The essay forces the student into impostor mode: pretending to know the university, pretending to be disinterested, pretending to be independent, pretending to be in control.

The flip side of this pretence is where the student does have a great deal of knowledge about the topic she/he is discussing, but has to pretend not to have this knowledge, for fear of being accused of plagiarism. In Part II I examine a tutor's response to a mature student who displays 'too much' knowledge, and the assumptions upon which this judgement rests. Clark and Ivanic (1997: 148) cite a student who gives a definition of utilitarianism in her essay, but points out in an interview that if she were an authority publishing an article in an academic journal, the definition would not be necessary, would in fact seem strange. Though she is a mature student with a life experience giving her much knowledge of the topic, she has to 'know her place' as a student and show that she understands a basic term.

All these tensions and pretences inherent in academic writing are exacerbated by the problem of prior authoritative discourses which conflict with the new authoritative discourses. Bakhtin's understanding of authority in discourses is one in which we encounter the authoritative word

> with its authority already fused to it. The authoritative word is located in a distanced zone, organically connected with a past that is felt to be hierarchically higher. It is, so to speak, the word of the fathers. Its authority was already *acknowledged* in the past. It is a *prior* discourse. It is therefore not a question of choosing it from among other possible discourses that are its equal. It is given (it sounds) in lofty spheres, not those of familiar contact.

> (1981: 342)

Authoritative discourse comes into conflict with 'internally persuasive' discourse, which is 'half ours and half someone else's' (Bakhtin, 1981: 345) and with which there is much more possibility for creativity and flexibility than with authoritative discourse, which 'permits no play with its borders' (343). Authoritative discourse 'cannot be represented – it is only transmitted' (344). (This is the way I feel about Bakhtin at the moment, as the number of quotes indicates!)

Bakhtin sees authoritative and internally persuasive discourses as interacting forces, so that the 'ideological becoming' of an individual is a process which consists of a struggle between authoritative and internally persuasive discourses. In other words, the relationship between these two types of discourses is not unconnected with Bartholomae's ideas of finding a compromise between a personal history and the history of a discipline, an old authority and a new.

I suggest that the student, on entering the university, encounters apparently immutable authoritative discourses, with their authority (of lecturers, key theorists) 'fused' to them, and because of their location in a 'distanced zone', 'hierarchically higher' than their more familiar, internally persuasive discourses, is able only to transmit these, rather than represent them. Later on in their academic development, for some, these discourses *become* more internally persuasive, and a process of making one's own meaning with them, of 'playing with the borders', of representing them in one's own words, becomes possible. Although for Bakhtin authoritative discourses are fixed, and cannot be transformed, but only overturned, my interpretation is that for the new student, the discourses of academia *seem* fixed and rigid, and may not be tampered with, although of course they are in reality extremely dynamic. They not only, in their authority, may not be tampered with, but the student, because of her/his *distance* from these authoritative discourses, and because of the power of prior authoritative discourses, which have not yet been discarded, is not *able* to manipulate, transform or make them her/his own. Control of these powerful discourses is still out of reach, and the internally persuasive discourses, the persona of the student, are in transition.

The last approach to plagiarism in student writing which I would like to consider is of particular importance when considering the student who is learning in a second or third language. This is the role of memory and of formulaic language.

The role of memory and formulaic language in second-language acquisition: *learning combinations of steps*

A new dance is learnt piece by piece, maybe two or four bars at a time. Each section is repeated several times, and later the whole thing will be put together. One section may be repeated later in the dance, or in another dance, with other costumes and music. So it is with learning a language.

The role played by memory in learning and in writing, in a first or second language, is not well understood, and frequently relegated to a 'second-class' form of learning. An extreme example of the use of memory in writing, which later became a famous case of plagiarism, is in the well-known story of the deaf and blind Helen Keller, who was accused of plagiarism at the age of eleven! (Swann, 1994). Later Keller herself wrote of the 'promiscuous' way in which people spelled all kinds of books and stories onto her hand (in Swann, 57), which did not enable her to place boundaries around what she 'felt', as none of it was visible or audible to her. She 'saw' the world through language, and her mind worked in such a way that retention of an image meant retention of the language of that image. It is not surprising that she used bits of 'borrowed' language word for word in her own writing. More astonishing is that a small disabled child, who sent a gift of a story to a person of significance in her life, who then had it published, could be accused of monstrous deception, taken to court and traumatized by the event for the rest of her life. As Swann puts it, 'Where the problem seems to have arisen is in the way people wanted to see Helen as an original genius' (67). Pennycook (1996) suggests that there are levels of memorization, some of which deepen understanding, noting the way in which some groups of students, such as Asian students, are derided as rote learners whilst at the same time praised as outstanding academic achievers. Memory function and academic achievement are poorly understood: it may be that some rote learning is essential for any kind of communication in one's second language.

In a way, a person studying in an additional language is 'seeing' the subjects she/he is studying through that language, just as Helen Keller 'saw' through the words traced on her hand. The concepts learned are inextricably attached to the language in which they are learnt. This is true for those learning in their first language as well. But if a student does not have much flexibility in the additional language, then writing about the new concepts may necessitate using the words attached to that concept, and these may be memorized chunks, also known as formulaic language.

Weinert (1995) writes that definitions of formulaic language are

> generally expressed in terms of processes, and refer to multi-word or multi-form strings which are produced or recalled as a whole chunk, much like an individual lexical item, rather than being generated from individual lexical items/forms with linguistic rules.

(182)

Weinert shows that there is much evidence to suggest that at all levels of language learning, from beginner to advanced level, chunks of language are learned and reproduced word for word. Formulaic language is also present in the speech of native speakers as well as learners of an additional language. Weinert cites evidence of formulaic language being used as communicative, productive and learning strategies. She argues that language is a 'formulaic-creative continuum' (198), with a complex relationship between 'formulaic language and rules, between memory and analysis'.

When we require paraphrase from a student, how different from the original a paraphrase must be to be acceptable is usually not clear. When one is learning the language formulaically, how is one able to put it fully into one's 'own words'? Paraphrase is significantly more difficult for the student not writing in their own language, because they have fewer alternative constructions and a more restricted lexicon available to them, and because words are stored in memory and accessed by the learner in chunks.

In addition to these difficulties, in our emphasis on analysis and originality, we undervalue the role of memory in learning. The deprecation of rote-learning strategies is a familiar tune in South Africa. Memory plays a vital role in all learning, not least the learning of another language, and the production of learned chunks of language in a piece of academic writing may be an unconscious or conscious learning strategy, and not plagiarism.

Watch a group of children asked to move freely to music. They will watch each other, copy and get ideas from each other, use bits of dances they know, march like soldiers or fly like butterflies, leap like Baryshnikov, die like the dying swan, move their hips like Michael Jackson. All bits stored in memory, copied from somewhere, to create something new.

Developing authorial voice: *from trance dancing to breathing life into the dance*

Scollon (1995), in an analysis of plagiarism and ideology, with reference to intercultural discourse, analyses powerful taken-for-granted concepts of communication such as the Sender-Message-Receiver formula. He focuses on the person as communicator, citing what he calls 'eight problems in constructing "the author"' (6). I shall deal with only a few here. He uses Goffman's *Frame Analysis*, in which he defines three different aspects of the production of communication, called the *animator*, the *author* and the *principal*. The animator is 'the talking machine, a body engaged in acoustic activity . . . the individual active in the role of utterance production' (Goffman in Scollon, 1995: 6). This may not be the author. The author, in Goffman's definition, is 'Someone who has selected the sentiments that are being expressed and the words in which they are encoded' (in Scollon, 1995: 7). However, the author may not take responsibility for these words: the person who does so is the principal. Scollon demonstrates effectively that very seldom are the roles of animator, principal and author unified in one person. For instance, this book is being authored by me, with the feedback and help of some of my colleagues, yet some of the responsibility for it, the principal-ship, will be taken by my editors, as well as (perhaps) some suggestions for actual wording (authoring). On publication in the Real Language Series, Pearson Education takes on some of the principalship (the act of publica-tion assumes some responsibility for the quality of the publication) and its final animation would rest with the production staff, cover designers and printers, etc. employed by the publishers. Using dance to illustrate, the author would be the choreographer, the principal the director, and the animators the dancers.

Interesting in this framework is how, in academic writing, the question of authorship of sources cited, and the stance to the views cited (the principal-ship) are signalled. When considering student learning, this is of significance for both reading and writing: in reading for detecting the voices and the author's stance to the voice present in a reading. Quotation marks and references establish authorship, but principalship is established through what Goffman calls 'laminator verbs' such as 'maintains', 'shows', 'on the con-trary' (in Scollon, 1995: 7). These stances are very subtly indicated through choice of words ('maintains' has a different stance from 'demonstrates'), so for someone reading in a language which is not their own, the principalship will not be easy to detect. Similarly, in writing, the subtle control of other texts and authors, and the writer's stance towards them, indicating author and principal for the reader, is a highly complex task.

Foucault (1984), who himself cites the work of great philosophers with nothing other than a name, and never seems to cite any modern authors, sees the emergence of authors as closely related to the time when authors could be punished, when ownership and copyright benefited and limited the actions of authors. He reverses the traditional idea of the author, who is normally seen as 'the genial creator of a work in which he deposits, with infinite wealth and generosity, an inexhaustible world of significations' (1984: 118). Foucault rejects this, maintaining that the author carries the societal function of limiting meaning, excluding and selecting, shutting out the terrifying proliferation of meaning of today. He predicts a time when the author functions will disappear, and

> all discourses would then develop in the anonymity of a murmur. We would no longer hear the questions that have been rehashed for so long: Who really spoke? Is it really he and not someone else? With what authenticity or originality? And what part of his deepest self did he express in his discourse? Instead, there would be other questions, like these: What are the modes of existence of this discourse? Where has it been used, how can it circulate, and who can appropriate it for himself? What are the places in it where there is room for possible subjects? Who can assume these various subject functions? And behind all these questions, we would hear hardly anything but the stirring of an indifference: What difference does it make who is speaking?
>
> (1984: 119)

I believe that it does make a difference who is speaking. Foucault himself is one to whose words and authorship we are not indifferent. Foucault was an agent whose tools of analysis have enabled many to look at the nature of the subject and the way it is constituted in a new way. His meanings were new, original, though his work must have been shaped by, and contained, many discourses and many other authors. Giddens (1987) finds poststructuralist thought fundamentally lacking a theory of human agency, and, regarding the notion of the author, he writes:

> Writing is sometimes portrayed as though texts wrote themselves; the relegation of the author to the role of a shadowy adjunct to writing is manifestly unsatisfactory. We can accept the significance of the theme of the decentring of the subject, and therefore the need to construct what an author is. But we shall have no proper grasp of the process of writing unless we manage to recombine satisfactorily the elements that have been decentred.
>
> (211)

The notion of authorship is in flux. Concepts of originality, of ownership of meaning and wording are complex and not adequately dealt with in much of our thinking about plagiarism, and our dealing with it in the academic context. But the author is not 'dead'. The author is alive, wriggling around in the complex contexts of the voices of others, and in the intersecting orchestras of power, but nevertheless making meaning from and in these voices.

Bakhtin knows that there is such a thing as an authorial presence, an agency within writing, that plays with, speaks to and within the voices of others. It is unsuccessful, incoherent writing that does not have this authorial presence. In a novice academic essay the voice of the author may not sound, and this has to do, as I have tried to show, with questions of the authority of the voices of others, and the lack of authority of the writer, the complicated masks and costumes of the genres of academic writing which are not made explicit, the alien nature of the discourses of academia, the hybridization of new and old discourses, and the formulaic nature in which language is learned and reproduced.

The voicelessness (a kind of trance dancing where the dancer is 'absent') of novice academic writing may also have to do with an obsession with an avoidance of plagiarism: for instance, as Thesen (1994) has found, the student may overuse reporting clauses such as 'he says', 'he went on to say', in order to scrupulously separate out what is his and what is the source. The penalties of plagiarism force a consciousness of borrowing and owing, which may be experienced as paralysing. Thus in the pursuit of scrupulous avoidance of plagiarism, the authorial voice may be lost in a multiplicity of attributions to others. This does not have to be, but gaining authority in academic writing means learning how to use the voices of others to develop one's own.

> One's own discourse and one's own voice, although born of another or dynamically stimulated by another, will sooner or later begin to liberate themselves from the authority of the other's discourse.
>
> (Bakhtin, 1981: 348)

The choreographer chooses from what she knows from others: music, forms of dance, steps, costumes, lighting, dancers. The more forms of dance she controls, and the more exposure to and learning of movement techniques, the more sophisticated her dancers, the more choice she has. In the perfect execution, the dancers carry out the vision of the choreographer, but they are each shaped by their own histories: where they have danced, who they have trained with, who they are. The choreographer has to know these dancers, take their individual attributes into account and work with them to create a whole, and know the discourses of the audience as well. It is an intricate, complex task. So it is with authors and words.

Notes

1. Recchio (1991) conducts an analysis similar to Thesen's using Bakhtin's understandings of intersecting discourses.
2. Peirce (1995) uses Bourdieu (1991) to show how power relationships construct the second language learner's right to speak and to be heard. I first drew on and extended her use of Bourdieu's 'legitimate discourse' in Angélil-Carter (1997). These ideas are used and further extended here.

A Multivoiced Text:
The Chorus

6

Introduction to Part II

Part II reports on the struggles of students in forging their own voices in their writing while using source texts, and the reflections and methods of academic staff regarding plagiarism and referencing. A short summary of the research process will give the reader a context for the voices presented in this section.

In the first phase of the research, all the assignments of one student, whom I call Tshediso, in his two writing subjects, were studied over one year. He and the tutors[1] who had marked his essays were interviewed. The data from this student's writing and interviews were particularly rich, as they showed his development over a year. The next phase took place in one Social Sciences department, which I shall call Department S. I analysed essays at first- and third-year level, mostly those which showed signs of difficulty in the complex task of synthesizing the words and views of others into an essay which had a 'voice'. However, I also examined some essays which were judged to be successful in terms of how source texts had been integrated into an argument. I interviewed students as well as the tutors and lecturers who had marked their assignments, in order to obtain a multi-faceted, interactive view of the learning environment with respect to writing and plagiarism (interactive in the sense of the different kinds of data feeding into one another, and producing new or modified research questions through-out the process). Essays, handbooks and interview data all formed the basis for an analysis of the problem of plagiarism in student academic writing. There was also a process of feedback to the research participants, and the department in which the research took place, as well as wider dissemination across the university and in conference papers.

The analysis presented here represents my selection and interpretation of relevant data from many essays and interviews, with students and staff. Using Lather's (1991) framework, the methodology used was postpositivist, inter-pretive, praxis-oriented, making use of some deconstructive methods. The analysis sought to probe deeply into the issues of plagiarism, and students' struggles around referencing in academic writing, and to provide a triangulated grid, a set of perspectives from the vantage points of students, lecturers, and tutors. This grid was supplemented by a discourse analysis of the departmental handbook, discussed in the next chapter. A central voice is, of course, my own, in what I as interviewer chose to focus on in interviews, in what I have selected from the data to present in this book, and in the way in which I have structured it and commented upon it.

I realize, in reflecting on my selection of data, that it is the voices of students that I have been most concerned to represent; it is their experiences with the practices of academic literacy that are least understood, I think, and need to be heard. It is also their experiences and struggles that to me are most revealing of the difficulties inherent in academic writing, and their words which bring to light old difficulties and raise new ones for academics to think about. However, all of the interviews with staff, as well as workshops we did with various staff members to report and reflect on the research, and the feedback that we received from colleagues all over the institution on articles which I and a colleague wrote in the university newspaper, raised new questions and new ways of thinking about the research problems for me. Although these voices may not be directly reflected in this chapter, they were extremely formative in my own thinking. As I write, therefore, I think of my audience as those who may be embedded in or struggling with the practices of academic literacy, and see myself as interpreter of a small corner of student experience, focused, however, to refract onto wider academic literacy practices.

In the following chapters, I will attempt to answer the following questions:

1. How do students, tutors and staff understand the role of referencing in academic writing?
2. What consequences do the practice of referencing and the monitoring of plagiarism have with regard to authority and voice in student writing?
3. What might be happening when students are thought to be plagiarizing?
4. What are the difficulties experienced in developing an authorial voice when using multiple sources?

The first question, examined in Chapter 8, attempts to explore the differences across lecturers and tutors in how the role of referencing is understood. It also attempts to explore the way in which students perceive this role, and how this confirms or contradicts what staff members believe its role to be. From an exploration of the role of referencing, I move in Chapter 9 on to what is actually happening, in terms of student authority and voice, regarding the practice of referencing, and what the negative and positive consequences of its enforcement and its focus may be. The third question, discussed in Chapter 10, probes in practice the question which is extensively explored in theory in Chapter 5, and attempts to support the theory through the words and writing of the students. The exploration tries to provide an alternative explanation for 'plagiarism', which has little to do with the immorality and dishonesty with which it is associated in the handbook. The final chapter of Part II, Chapter 11, attempts to examine an oft-neglected side of the use of multiple voices in texts, i.e. how the author inserts herself (or does not do so) into the writing, and signals (or fails to signal) her stance in relation to the writers she has used to support her argument. I hope to show that referencing, and the elements of academic practice that underlie it, play a central role in academic writing, but that this role is underestimated, and might be put to much greater use in the curriculum than the negative role that is often presently assigned to it.

You will notice that the students have names (not their own) and I have told a little of their life stories. I am conscious that these brief summaries tell us very little about their identities: there is much left out, and identity is never single or fixed, but always multiple and in flux, so these portraits are of necessity flawed. However, I want to give the reader just a flavour of who the students are. Unfortunately I have not felt it possible to tell the histories of academic staff members, fascinating as they are. An understanding of something of their lives helped me to understand their approach to writing, but I felt it would make them too easily identifiable – some of them being public figures – if I included this in the analysis. Likewise with the tutors. I did not want anything they said to work against them in any way: they may well have been heading for academic careers in the department in which they were tutoring.

Note

1. Tutors at the University of Cape Town are usually postgraduate students doing a Masters or Honours degree in the discipline who work part-time for the department. Occasionally, however, third-year students are used. Tutors lead small-group tutorials and mark student essays. Lecturers are full-time academics whose duties include conducting lectures and setting exams and essays. They sometimes also lead a tutorial group and mark essays.

7

Plagiarism and referencing as communicated in a departmental handbook: *a discourse analysis*

This chapter contains a brief discourse analysis of the first-year departmental handbook of Department S, as a typical handbook within the Social Sciences, focusing on the section on referencing and plagiarism. A departmental handbook is a text which represents a particular point of communication between staff and students, often mediated by tutors. In using discourse analysis I sought to uncover the understandings of plagiarism and referencing which lie behind the language of the text, and to examine the way in which these are communicated to students. I draw on Fairclough's method of discourse analysis, as it is a thorough, powerful method, which I have made use of previously (Angélil-Carter and Murray, 1996) and which is very clearly set out in Fairclough (1992). The categories I have used are drawn from his framework. I briefly discuss the overall functions and purpose of the handbook as a discourse practice, the conditions of its production and consumption, and the link which it forms in an intertextual chain, and then turn to the sections on plagiarism and referencing, and examine coherence and metaphor in the actual wording. In the concluding chapter of this book, I make some alternative suggestions for what might be pedagogically useful to include in communication with students about plagiarism and citation. The first of Fairclough's categories which I discuss is the overall discourse practice of the handbook.

Discourse practice

The discourse practice refers to the wider social practice of the discourse under analysis, its particular social function or role. A handbook is essentially an introduction for the student into the department and the curriculum: at best it gives explicit instructions to the apprentice to the discipline on some of the codes and conventions of the discipline, as well as presenting an overview of the course, deadlines for essays, etc. The handbook's genre is that of the university departmental handbook, and it acts as mediator/communicator between department and students. In the absence of other kinds of mediation, it may be for students the only means of finding out about referencing conventions in the department, and what constitutes plagiarism.

The conditions of discourse practice

Here one needs to examine the 'social practices of text production and consumption associated with the type of discourse the sample represents' (Fairclough, 1992: 233). In terms of production, it is interesting to consider Goffman's 'animator, principal and author' divisions, discussed in Chapter 5 (Goffman in Scollon, 1995: 6). There are no authors mentioned anywhere in the handbook, and, as far as I understand it, the handbook is a very collaborative effort, consisting of revisions of old handbooks, borrowings from other departments' handbooks, and inputs from a number of different staff members. It is thus difficult to establish authorship. The animator would be the person who finally puts this piece of work into print, and this would be one of the support staff. Who the principal is, i.e. who takes responsibility for the whole, however, is not clear in a reading of the handbook as it stands, although from my experience of the department I have a fair idea of who this would be. In terms of consumption, it is my belief, judging from my interviews and experience with students, that unless they are specifically referred to the handbook in various fora, they might perhaps read through it once, and then put it aside. The handbook has to be effectively mediated in order to be comprehended, first, and in order to be acted upon.

Intertextual chains

This denotes how a discourse sample is distributed, and from which texts it is transformed or into which it transforms itself. Interesting to note here is that the section on essay guidelines, of which this extract is a part, was partly 'borrowed' from another department, which is acknowledged at the end of the handbook. It is not clear which parts were used.

The goal of the section on referencing is, I presume, that it be translated into effective referencing in the essays of students, and avoidance of plagiarism. My interviews with students indicated that many of them read the handbook only cursorily, and that if they did, they did not find it adequate in explaining when to reference, and how to indicate which is their voice and which are those of the sources. Two of the students whom I interviewed who had written good essays, however, said that they learnt how to reference through using the handbook. This says something about the motivation of these students, but perhaps also about to whom the handbook communicates, and to whom it does not. I now move on to some of the actual wording of the extract below:

Plagiarism means that another writer's words and/or opinions have been used <u>without being acknowledged.</u> This occurs when someone else's work has been copied word for word, or in a slightly altered form, and there are no quotation marks and/or references to show that these <u>words</u> have been
5   borrowed. Plagiarism also occurs when the <u>ideas</u> of another writer have been used but this has not been indicated in references. It is regarded as a VERY SERIOUS OFFENCE.

<u>REFERENCES:</u>
In preparing your work you are relying heavily on writing and research
10   by others. Yet your paper must be your own work and you may not present the ideas and data of others as if they are your own. The solution is to acknowledge scrupulously whatever sources you have used.

This is a moral issue: honest authors do not present others' information and words as though they are their own. To do so is to commit the form
15   of intellectual theft known as plagiarism, a serious offence which could possibly lead to exclusion from the university. In your reading you will become acquainted with various conventions for references, or different ways of acknowledgement by authors of their use of others' information and words.

20   The departmental rules on this matter are the following:

1. Acknowledge your use of the ideas and information of others by placing a reference at the end of the appropriate phrase, sentence, collection of sentences, or paragraph. Stated differently, when you use the ideas and information of others, but express these in your own words, you must
25   use reference. To paraphrase something does not make it your own work, and you are obliged to acknowledge your source.

Coherence

According to Fairclough, one of the questions to consider here is 'how ambivalent is the text for particular interpreters, and consequently how much inferential work is needed?' (1992: 233). As a reader, I am somewhat uneasy with lines 1 to 5. This is the first half of what seems to be a definition of plagiarism: 'Plagiarism means that another writer's words and/or opinions have been used without being acknowledged. This occurs when someone else's work has been copied word for word, or in a slightly altered form, and there are no quotation marks and/or references to show that these <u>words</u> have been borrowed.' The first uncertainty comes with the word 'slightly'. This seems to imply that if the words are *considerably* altered without referencing then it is not plagiarism, so that skilful paraphrase without acknowledgement would be acceptable. The next ambivalence comes with the use of 'and/or' in line 4. Clearly in the case of close copying of another writer's words, there should be quotation marks *and* references. However by inserting 'or', there seems to be a possibility that one might have a situation where quotation marks are needed, but no references. In fact, there are situations where references are needed without quotation marks, but this is not when actual words have been borrowed. This sentence is clearly referring to the use of actual words, as is indicated by the underlining of *words* in line 4. The use of the word 'or' confuses. A definition needs to be carefully thought out and stated in a manner that enables new students and students whose home language is not English to understand. It is interesting that there is no mention here of the usual definition of plagiarism as the *intention to deceive*, as discussed in Chapter 3.

Metaphor

Under this heading I would like first to examine the metaphor of 'borrow' used in line 5. 'Borrow' means to obtain something on loan from somebody else, with the intention of giving it back to the lender. The word can, however, be somewhat loosely used, as a politeness strategy, when there is no expectation of returning an item which is of little value. The metaphor is often used in connection with plagiarism. It is less weighty than the metaphor of theft, which is also used frequently in this connection, and is to be found here in line 15. Borrowing implies permission to take, whilst theft connotes taking without permission. Neither is appropriate to plagiarism, because when appropriating ideas or words from others we are not depriving them of their words or thoughts, as the thief (or borrower, temporarily) deprives us of our property. The borrower of words and ideas has no way or intention of giving them back. The use of the word 'offence' (lines 8 and 15) extends the criminal metaphor inherent in the idea of theft. The capitals of 'VERY SERIOUS OFFENCE' in line 7, and the warning of the possible punishment for plagiarism of exclusion from the university (line 16), send an intimidating message to the student reader, as does the statement in lines 13–14 that 'This is a moral issue: honest authors do not present others' information and words as though they are their own'. There are many difficulties here, merely in those words 'present others' information and words as though they are their own'. These are the difficulties of the first-year student for whom most information about the discipline is *not* their own, they are the difficulties of paraphrase, and the use of discipline-specific terms or phrases, and the problem of the second-language learner who is using memory to reproduce language formulaically, as discussed in Chapter 5. All of these difficulties will emerge in the essay and interview data in the following chapters. In the assertion that this is a moral issue is the shamefulness of the deed of plagiarism, and the lack of honesty of the offender: plagiarism as fraud. Once again, as in the letter to the *Monday Paper* reproduced in Chapter 1, there is no sense that the problem of plagiarism could be anything other than wilful fraud.

This departmental handbook, then, projects plagiarism as an undisputed, deceitful and immoral act, although it acknowledges in lines 9 to 12, in that little word 'yet', the contradiction in 'relying heavily on writing and research by others' and 'your paper must be your own work'. It also gives a range of examples of how to acknowledge sources, to which I shall return in the final chapter, when I make some suggestions for an alternative approach to plagiarism and referencing which might be included in a departmental handbook.

8

The role of referencing

not to steal the words . . .
they might be impressed . . .
purely gymnastic . . .
teachers replicating themselves in their students . . .
about crediting, about line of argument and identifying line of
argument, tradition.

As stated in Chapter 1, it is my intention to show that plagiarism is a disputed concept, and that many instances of 'plagiarism' in student academic writing are not instances of intentional 'dishonesty', 'theft' or 'immorality', but problems of academic literacy. I believe that the voices of students in interviews and essays which I present in this and the following chapters demonstrate this quite clearly. This chapter looks at the question: how do students, tutors and academic staff understand the role of referencing in academic writing?

Students overwhelmingly understand that the role of referencing is one of display of coverage of the readings, of indicating for the tutor that you have read the required readings, or perhaps read more than the required readings. Some of them, in addition, understand it to be a matter of accreditation of source, and in particular they think its role is the avoidance of plagiarism.

Mangaliso is a first-year student whose secondary education was severely disrupted due to his role in the self defence units (SDUs) on the East Rand in the two years prior to the first democratic elections in 1994. His essay was selected because large sections of it seemed to have been plagiarized, and for him the role of referencing is the avoidance of plagiarism, the need to credit, and display of knowledge:

S.   What is the role of referencing in the academic essay? Why is it required?

M. In my view?

S. Ja, in your view.

M. Okay. I think it's to make sure that, eh as they told us, not to steal the words from other academics again, because we have to acknowledge that.

S. Okay what do you mean by 'steal the words from' – where does that come from? You said somebody told you that? Who told you that?

M. Yes. In the document they gave us, the red booklet, in the first semester in Political Studies, which says that quite categorically that you may not steal the words of other academics again – we have to acknowledge the sources. Which I think is a good thing. You cannot expect the other person writing a book – without acknowledging those words.

S. So if you take the words of somebody else without acknowledging then you're stealing in some way?

M. Yes.

S. So you've got to avoid that. Why else do you think it's required?

M. The referencing? Oh to show – it indicates that you have read much books, and you give perhaps the impression, that you've consulted as many books as possible. Yes and I think that that also does encourage you at some point to read more books.

S. The referencing? The fact that you have to reference encourages you to read. Just explain how that works?

M. Yes because – eh if some, if you're writing an essay therefore, ne? that will enrich the knowledge that you have, that will show also the deep understanding of the essay that you're writing, it will reflect your strength that you have read many books and also you've understood those books of which you are reading there.

After checking whether I want *his* view (does this mean that his view contradicts what he has been told about its role?), the first thing that Mangaliso mentions is the avoidance of plagiarism. He understands the use of the words of others without acknowledgement as theft, a metaphor he relates directly back to the Political Studies handbook. He agrees with this policy and does not question the notion of plagiarism as a criminal activity. His second reason is to 'show that you have read much books' and, a subtle shift, to 'give perhaps *the impression* that you've consulted as many books as possible'. Thus referencing as display of readings covered becomes referencing as containing the possibility of *false display* of readings covered, a shift which lies in the word 'impression'. He also relates referencing to understanding, saying, 'that will enrich the knowledge that you have, that will show also the deep understanding of the essay that you're writing, it will reflect your strength that you have read many books and also you've understood those books of which you are reading there.' So Mangaliso seems to move quite directly from referencing as display of coverage, to display of understanding. The important thing for the moment is not whether referencing can display understanding, but how Mangaliso understands its role, as both display of coverage and display of understanding. Mangaliso's need to impress, his awareness of his lack of authority in the discourse, and of the authority of the sources, leads him to plagiarism. (Mangaliso was the one student whom I suspected of plagiarism in the real sense, of deliberate deception, of all the students that I interviewed.)

Emma is a British student who was doing a third-year course in Department S, as part of a postgraduate Diploma. She has an undergraduate degree from Cambridge. She went to a private girls' school in London, and a sixth form college for A-levels. She read history for three years. She came to South Africa to fill in time while her Cambridge supervisor was on sabbatical, and because she loves Third World studies. She is most enthusiastic about her studies, and very knowledgeable about her field. She has kept a diary for the past four years in which she notes international events in the media. She used this diary when writing her essay ('. . . When I noticed that practically every country in Africa was wising up for democracy, I seemed to be literally the only person in England that noticed these things, you know, so I started writing them down so that I'd know that I wasn't the one who was completely insane'). Her essay was not selected for referencing problems by the marker; it was given to me with the remark that it was the best essay seen thus far, and did I want to have a look at it. It turned out to be one of the most interesting in terms of referencing practices, and I asked Emma to come to an interview. Emma claimed never to have heard about referencing until she came to the University of Cape Town, as it was never an issue at Cambridge. In the following extract from her interview, she too sees the role of referencing as avoidance of plagiarism, and for verification purposes:

S.   What do you think the role of referencing is in an academic essay?
E.   I suppose in part it's to stop you plagiarizing, so that when you write down someone's idea at least you know and the person who's marking it knows that that's where you originally got it from.
S.   Was that an issue at Cambridge? Plagiarism?
E.   Heavens no not at all.
     . . .
S.   Anything else about the role of referencing?
E.   Must be useful for them in some way, since they want you to put down the page number – damn nuisance – so it must be useful for them to see if you've grasped the idea or mangled it.

Emma seems to see the usefulness of referencing chiefly as making the monitoring/policing role of the marker easier. Referencing stops you from plagiarizing, so that you and the marker know where the idea comes from. Although she seems to see some usefulness for the writer in this first part, in the second answer the use of 'them' marks an oppositional stance: she is distancing herself from any notion of usefulness, it's a 'damn nuisance', and the only reason she can see for why the page number is required, is that it must be so that the marker can check the accuracy of your interpretation.

Tshediso[1] is the student who was interviewed over a period of a year. He is a mature first-year student who matriculated[2] in 1986. He lived in Botswana for eighteen months, and when he returned began organizing underground structures for the African National Congress (ANC).[3] He was arrested and tried, conducting his own defence at his trial, and was sentenced to eight years' imprisonment. In prison he studied through UNISA,[4] and became the prison librarian and the chairperson of the recreation committee. He was granted indemnity and released from prison in 1991. Tshediso has this to say about the role of referencing in academic writing:

T.   Well, I think, in a way it's to acknowledge somebody else's work because if you don't reference then it means you are using somebody else's, his ideas as if they are your own.

S.   Okay.

T.   And I think it gives even, it gives more impetus to your paper, it would show that you have used the other source, you did not rely on what you know.

S.   So you think that for somebody reading it, when they see the referencing they know that you –

T.   They might be impressed . . .

S.   They might be impressed.

There are many other instances of students' understanding of referencing as avoidance of plagiarism, referencing as a means of monitoring or policing, and particularly referencing as display, in the interview data. The handbook in Department S endorses the negative view of referencing as avoidance of plagiarism, when it states: 'The solution is to acknowledge scrupulously whatever sources you have used. This is a moral issue: honest authors do not present others' information and words as though they are their own. To do so is to commit the form of intellectual theft known as plagiarism.' The message that students seem to be receiving is either that referencing has the negative role of an avoidance of plagiarism and a means of monitoring students' reading, or that the role of referencing is to demonstrate to the marker that you have read, and how much you have read, and even, in Mangaliso's case, the depth of understanding of what you have read. Taking this latter role to its logical conclusion, a student may easily believe that the more you reference, the more you've covered, and the better your marks will be. This is the conclusion that my next respondent, Lindiwe, came to.

Lindiwe is a first-year student who went to a previously 'Coloured',[5] Afrikaans-medium school for a while, but left because of transport problems and because she struggled with Afrikaans (her third language) there. She matriculated at a relatively good Western Cape township school. At UCT she was not involved in anything other than her studies. She hopes to have a career in Public Administration. Lindiwe wrote an essay which was full of long quotes and very closely paraphrased pieces from the readings. When I asked her why this was so, she said,

L. Like my tutor usually says if you didn't reference, she is not going to mark your essays. Or else if you didn't reference, she's going to deduct 10% before she marks. So I just tell myself ooo! I've got to reference, I've got no choice.

This emphasis led Lindiwe to believe that the more she referenced, and the more closely she drew from the readings, the better her essay would be:

L. I think that as this was my first essay to write, so I felt that I should include in my essay more references, so that, I thought it was the only way to attract the marker.
S. Why did you feel that?
L. Because as she was explaining referencing to us, it seemed to me the most important thing, the most important thing when you are writing an essay. So I felt that I should give references, and I should use all those readings that she gave us.
S. So you felt the more you showed that you've read and the more you reference –
L. The more I'm going to get good marks.

None of the messages that the students are getting, it seems to me, are particularly sound pedagogical reasons for referencing. If there are important pedagogical reasons for referencing, and I shall argue in the concluding chapter that there are, then these were not being made explicit to students, or if they were, then students did not find them convincing. One student who did not is Mandisi.

Mandisi, a third-year student, was educated in a fairly well-resourced Catholic school in the Orange Free State. His father is a senator in the present government, and Mandisi himself has done a great deal of public speaking in various public forums. His essay was given to me by the lecturer with the remark that the essay was brilliant, and any academic would be proud of having done this analysis herself, but there were no references. At the end of his essay the marker wrote: 'This is an excellent exposition and why oh why is it not properly referenced. Please resubmit with proper referencing so that I can give you the 80% you certainly should have. By not referencing you strip it of its academic value and you lose its value both for yourself and the audience i.e. myself as reader.'

Mandisi came across in the interview as clearly knowledgeable and articulate, but resistant to certain aspects of academia, and one of them is referencing.

> *M.* The thing is that I have a problem also with that idea, this whole preoccupation with referencing . . .
>
> *S.* You see it as a preoccupation?
>
> *M.* I see it as something that is required.
>
> *S.* What's your problem with it?
>
> *M.* To some extent, it's like – you know this method – in Afrikaans poetry they use this intertextual method, which says that you as an individual are a text, so to me you are a product of differing forces, in fact you –
>
> *S.* So you're saying that you're a product of different forces acting on you as a text?
>
> *M.* [inaudible] so it's actually interactional – your environment, elements in your being are text. The interaction of extrinsic and intrinsic factors constitute you as a text.
>
> *S.* So now relate this to referencing.
>
> *M.* Referencing to some extent denies this, because I have to refer. And some of the things I cannot, I know that I use other people's . . . I cannot be able to go back and point out from what source I got it.
>
> *S.* You cannot point out . . . And why not?
>
> *M.* Because some – they may have been informal discussions, like a person's point or something, you don't know the page, you don't know the name of the author . . .
>
> *S.* In that case would you be taking that idea and holding it in your memory?
>
> *M.* Yes. You won't write it down but you remember it.

He quoted Freire, saying there is a continuum of education for liberation to education for enslavement. He saw referencing as part of a 'conditioning of attitude' to take a certain place in society, and spoke of the system of ideas as commodities, for profit. He has never thought it important to reference, and says that in the courses he has done it has never been emphasized. The following discussion exemplifies his approach:

> *S.* When you're writing essays do you find referencing easy or difficult?
>
> *M.* I have never paid particular attention to this. In '92 I bought a book on punctuation and referencing by Visser, I think it's a standard document.
>
> *S.* On referencing? Punctuation and referencing?

M. Yes – punctuation and referencing. I was doing English 1 at the time and they recommended it. But I never really used it – I tried but there was no stimulus to try to use it to reference.

S. Okay why?

M. I don't know, I bought it but I really didn't use it.

S. So you just never regarded referencing –

M. As important, as that important. Although I see it's important, but to me there was no stimulus. So I tend to regard this referencing as a by-product, something you must do at the end. That is unfortunate although I do, I do acknowledge that it's important. But most of the time I do it at the end and you find that at the end there's not much time, not enough time to do it properly.

Although he seems to feel some pressure to acknowledge the importance of referencing, it is clear from what he says and how he behaves (referencing only at the end, never paying attention to the book he bought) and by what he says (it's 'a by-product', 'there was no stimulus to try to use it', 'I have never paid particular attention to this') that he regards it as trivial. His essay bears this out: he obviously has no sense of how to reference; on the few occasions where he does so, it is technically completely incorrect.

Mandisi has either chosen deliberately to ignore referencing, because he finds it insignificant, it has never been emphasized in his courses, and because it is part of a wider system of education to which he is resistant, or its value has never been explained to him in a way that makes it seem important enough to take some trouble over. His marker, S3, in discussing his essay, says:

S3. . . . they come to UCT, they come to do a course, they do a course in S., the University of Cape Town regards me capable of developing, of offering a course, if they wish to run a counter to my course, please give themselves a credit and do so with pleasure. We can then have a competition, we can then see who's going to get the accreditation. I mean this is not about a licence to teach. And I'm more than happy to engage in a debate or discussion through the vehicle of essays with him. Read my material and tell me why you think your stuff is better.

S. Okay, if he was to put that – locate it within your material – then you would be happy.

S3. And I would like him to reference the stuff. Because he's not sucking it out of his thumb.

S. And if he's getting it from, I mean this is what he told me, he said, it's discussions outside in political fora . . .

S3. Well then, I want to know, then I want – Well he needs to be paying attention. He must say, I went to an SACP[6] meeting in May 19 – what I'm saying is if he is going to regard these things as contributing to his education, he needs to become like Emma, but instead of the radio, he needs to be writing these things down and have a record of it. He's then able to say to me, 25th June 1994, SACP discussion Mowbray, Bongo Bongo said da da da, the debate raged around these issues, this has immediate bearing on this essay.

So this staff member is insistent that all information needs to be sourced, to the extent of the political discussion held in an SACP meeting. I believe, from looking at the way that this person marks, that S3 wishes to inculcate scholarly habits, and would not, in fact, insist that every single piece of information be referenced. What she is looking for, rather, is that the student has covered her readings, and she would then permit outside knowledge to be linked to that. However, it seems that in her interactions with students, this is not made clear. In a desire to develop in her students scholarly methods of recording information, the lecturer seems to be denying the possibility of independent, outside knowledge which can legitimately be included in an essay without referencing. This she seems to find threatening in this particular student, and seems to feel that her control is lost when outside sources are used ('We can then have a competition, we can then see who's going to get the accreditation', 'this is not about a licence to teach').

Rose, a tutor marking essays for the third-year course, puts the problem well:

> R. I mean people are saying intellectual theft all these things, you must be honest when you're writing your academic papers, I mean I think that people who are teaching students should be honest about the problems in defining things – not saying you're so ignorant that you don't know the facts. And be honest about the fact that things are disputed and if people are going to set guidelines then um then it should be done – I mean being able to spell out the guidelines. I think that one of the reasons why the guidelines aren't spelt out, is that there isn't a common understanding of what the guidelines mean, and then people get very confused.

So Rose is saying that issues of referencing and plagiarism are not clear cut at all, and rather than pretend that they are, it would be more valuable to acknowledge the difficulties, and spell them out in guidelines. She puts her finger on the problem when she says that 'there isn't a common understanding of what the guidelines mean', and here I take her to mean amongst staff. Another staff member, when thinking about why students find referencing difficult, concurs with this viewpoint:

> S1. Why do they have problems? Students have problems because we actually don't teach it, we give written instructions, but we don't

teach, we don't go through examples, we don't rationalize why, we say it's courtesy, we don't touch our hats, anymore, we don't touch our forelocks, we don't do that anymore, that was courtesy, no longer required, so we haven't yet articulated to students in a way that makes sense to them, why it's important. And I think the reason is because we haven't thought enough about it ourselves, it's an area we are not sure of, and it's much easier to just set up the rules, if you do, you do, if you don't you get punished. So we haven't done enough work, so in other words, we're at fault, it is as simple as that.

It seems clear, then, that the logic of referencing, the rationale for referencing, remains opaque to students, partly because it has not been 'articulated to students in a way that makes sense to them, why it's important'. This staff member thinks that courtesy, 'touching our forelocks', is no longer a convincing reason for referencing. The reason why the rationale given to students does not go further than this lies in the staff's lack of reflection about that rationale. Both this staff member, and another, S2, question the value of referencing at the undergraduate level:

> S2.　. . . so there are purposes where references are essential, I mean I would say, that it is perfectly reasonable to require referencing as per the Harvard method, or any other acceptable scholarly method, footnoting, at postgraduate level, I mean there is a reasonable presumption that at postgraduate level, people are participating in, or beginning to participate in, as it were, the debates that take place in the international community of scholars and that particular discipline. But, at undergraduate level, certainly, at first-year level, and certainly with the classes that I've got, the value that it has is purely, as I say, gymnastic.
>
> S.　It's a training.
>
> S2.　Ja, but not a very good one, I mean not a terribly useful one, I mean they might as well learn lists of prime numbers.

S2 sees a marked difference in the need for referencing at the undergraduate and postgraduate level. In tracing the reasons for why it is insisted upon in undergraduate writing he says:

> S2.　Now how it got into undergraduate curricula has to do with the view that it was part of preparing undergraduates to be scholars . . . because teachers imagine that they are actually trying to replicate themselves in their students, whereas, most undergraduates that I teach are not going to become academics. There is another view which I've never heard articulated, but I suspect is unconscious and may have merit, and that is, referencing is to writing as playing scales is to playing the piano.

> S.   Just practice.
>
> S2. Well, I mean, there is value in learning certain mechanical skills, I mean, I don't take the view that everything has to be spontaneous and colourful, and so on and so on, I mean, I think, it's a kind of intellectual gymnastics or academic gymnastics, which is of no value in itself. But is a kind of mind toughening, and, like most exercises, painful. So, I can see a point under that heading, in making students reference, and it's more or less the only reason I actually tolerate the insistence on referencing.

So generally S2 does not see any pedagogic value for referencing at undergraduate level, other than in behavioural, habit-forming terms. In other words, therefore, it seems reasonable to conclude that both S1 and S2 are unable to make explicit to students the rationale for referencing at the undergraduate level, because they themselves are sceptical of its usefulness at that level. S2 sees it as important that students work with texts and other people's ideas, but he separates referencing from this work, as the following extract indicates:

> S2. It is also a very easy thing to fudge, so students can make a bad essay look quite impressive, simply by learning the art of designing a bibliography and the Harvard referencing. But it can be an essay which has no thought, and I say, the real skills are to learn first of all how to read somebody else's ideas, and how to present them clearly and fairly, and then how to comment upon them independently. That seems to me what is by far the most useful career skill we can offer them, because that is a skill you need, whatever job you do, certainly whatever job you're doing, in the so-called age of information.

At various points in the interview, S2 mentions that he regards 'the business of referencing as the major disincentive to doing academic writing', most of it as 'either showing off or padding', as 'a modern bureaucratic fad this, it is a fetish, it is a fetish which is engaged in to substitute thinking', and nothing more than 'academic good manners'. It is not surprising, therefore, that with what could almost be described as a contempt for referencing, or, in the case of S1, the scepticism of its value at undergraduate level, students will see it as only display of coverage, avoidance of plagiarism, or accreditation for reasons of 'academic good manners', and nothing more.

S3 has a very different viewpoint. S3's instruction to students regarding citation on the essay information sheet was: 'Any student citing less than 5 readings will have their essay returned unmarked but noted for DP[7] purposes.' In an interview, she said the following:

S.   What is scholarship and how does it relate to citation?

S3. About crediting, about line of argument and identifying line of argument, tradition, I don't know how else to put it to you. It's intellectual tradition. It's the kind of thing I don't do it anymore that I used to do with students, where I would say to them, let's take the Liberals writing in 1930s and let's take the Marxist writings in 1930s, what are the positions they're holding, let's move to the 1970s when both the Liberals and Marxists understood the complexity of the interaction between class and race, so let's see that a synthesis is emerging, okay, where both class and race are being taken up, but they are understood in different ways in terms of framework.

S.   So it's about location in traditions.

S3. And for you to understand how you make breakthroughs. So that things that are polar opposites, because there is a big debate and people draw the lines sharply, okay, only the time – as you have more and more studies done, will come together . . . and that's a synthesis – I don't use those words you know – but from that synthesis is going to emerge new contradictions and new scripts, so that if we look at the post-Cold War period and say this is the defeat of the Marxist or Socialist tradition, my argument is it will re-emerge in a different way, but it is true that the liberal argument wiped it out in a particular moment in time.

S.   So what is scholarship then?

S3. It's identifying all that, it's participating in that, it's about forging new ways of thinking about the world, it's about deepening your knowledge, your analytical capacity.

So S3 relates citation to accreditation, but also to participating in debates, and understanding how intellectual traditions merge and differ, and how new ones emerge.

It is clear, then, that there is a distinct divergence between the way that S2 and S1 on the one hand, and S3 on the other, think about referencing, although the former do see its role differently at the postgraduate level. In the way that S3 speaks, it is clear that she tries to have her students understand that intellectual traditions move and change and interact with one another, and through citation students can locate thinkers and writers within these traditions. There is a gap between the way that S3 marks essays and the way she speaks, which will become clearer later. I have a sense, through meetings with S3, and from the way that she marked essays before the interviews, that S3's thinking about referencing had always been that it is a fairly technical skill, and a display of how much reading the student had done, and she had not, in fact, made the direct link between intellectual debates and citation before the research process began. This would go some way towards explaining the reasons for the difference in the interview and the essay data. It also helps to explain why the links she made in the interview are not evident in what her students say about referencing, though there may be many other reasons for this, a principal one being that it was simply not discussed during the lectures.

So referencing is seen by students as playing the roles of avoidance of plagiarism and monitoring of how sources are used, as display of coverage and display of understanding, as part of the general 'conditioning' that education performs. Academic staff saw citation as a purely 'gymnastic' and not very useful training, not appropriate at undergraduate level. For one staff member, however, for whom it also seemed to be a form of control, it is crucial to an understanding of the contexts of theories and debates.

Having looked at the divergent views on the role of referencing in academic writing, I move in the next chapter to the consequences of the practice of referencing, with regard to authority and voice, in student writing.

Notes

1. I am indebted to my colleague Tim Hughes for some of the details of Tshediso's story. Hughes also interviewed Tshediso, for other purposes, and this is reported in Shay, Bond and Hughes (1994).
2. Matriculation is the twelfth and final year of schooling.
3. The African National Congress was a powerful underground resistance movement in the apartheid era, and is now the present ruling government.
4. The University of South Africa, a distance learning university through which many political prisoners obtained their degrees.
5. The Nationalist Party classified South Africans into racial groups, one of which was known as 'Coloured', i.e. people of mixed race.
6. South African Communist Party.
7. Due Performance. In order to fulfil the requirements of a course, students have to obtain a Due Performance certificate, indicating that a certain number of assignments, etc. have been completed.

9

Consequences of the practice of referencing and the monitoring of plagiarism

Negative consequences

taking their authority away...

Somehow it is assumed that whatever you know that is tangible and constructive you must have read it somewhere. It is impossible that you might have heard it or you might have thought it on your own.

maybe I was thinking it's not common knowledge to him...

In this chapter I explore what the practice of referencing and the monitoring of plagiarism as practices actually do, both in a positive and a negative sense. The question asked here is: what consequences do the practice of referencing and the monitoring of plagiarism have with regard to authority and voice in student writing? I begin with some of the negatives, starting with Tshediso:

> *T.* And one other thing, sometimes you do find ideas in somebody else's work whilst you already have known about these things so why should I reference – I've known it before I read about it.
>
> ...
>
> *S.* How do you know it?
> *T.* Well – I would categorize that as common knowledge, so those are things that you get when you speak to people in some cases you hear on the radio – on the news, and on the TV – you read in the newspaper, you won't even remember at some stages on which magazine did I find this.
> *S.* So what do you do then in those cases now when you feel that it is your own – common knowledge as you say?

T.   I present, I present it as mine.

S.   You do?

T.   I present it as mine, because for example I cannot reference my friend.

S.   If you wanted to reference your friend, I mean when you have used your friend's words or ideas –

T.   No I wouldn't know because if for example we are having a verbal exchange I would be giving ideas and he would be teaching in some as well so it's an interaction and I wouldn't know at the end of the day who said this and who said this.

S.   Okay, so then you – what you do is present it as yours, now is that acceptable? Do you find that tutors accept that, the markers of your essay?

T.   I, I think that when they mark they concentrate on the prescribed works that is when they see something I think they look again on the prescribed work – is this thing mentioned?
     . . . Normally what I've done – what I've started doing now is to use the prescribed works only, that's what I've attempted to do particularly with my latest essays in [Department S].

S.   Do you use the prescribed works only?

T.   I'm trying to do so because when you come up with your own examples and your own ideas then it is assumed that you are plagiarizing – simply because there is no referencing. Somehow it is assumed that whatever you know that is tangible and constructive you must have read it somewhere. It is impossible that you might have heard it or you might have thought it on your own.

So Tshediso's response to the way his own knowledge, and his use of outside sources, has been discounted is to shut out what he knows, and to stick with the prescribed readings only. He points out that the printed word is privileged ('It is impossible that you might have heard it'), and that independent thought is not expected ('It is impossible that you might have . . . thought it on your own').

The role of prior knowledge in constructivist learning theory is well established: it is crucial that the learner's present understanding is taken into account and incorporated into the new learning. As Tshediso's words imply, the practice of referencing is perhaps working against learning, in shutting out prior knowledge, and even encouraging students not to seek knowledge which is outside of the prescribed reading list – a direction which I think few academics would want their students to take. (Tshediso's decision on this is evident in his subsequent essays, where he did in fact incorporate only the prescribed readings, and limited his 'unreferenceable' examples, though he did incorporate one that I noticed, and was not asked to reference it, perhaps a reflection of his developing authority as an academic writer.)

With regard to the privileging of the printed word; this is an interesting aspect to referencing in the age of information explosion through computer technology and the media. It is my belief that we have not yet begun to know how to deal adequately with the kinds of information that students now have access to, beyond their course readings. One tutor, Lyn, emphasizes referencing a great deal in her tutorials and feedback to students. So much so that her students came up with references for the lecture notes, their history teachers, and Lyn herself. When I told Lyn about a student who was asked to reference examples he had gathered from the media to illustrate his argument, she stated categorically that he should have used other examples that he could have documented in some way by going to the library and finding printed documentation. Later on in the interview she elaborates:

> *L.*   I think it goes back to the whole thing that I said about, don't use the example if you can't empirically reference it. It's safer for us to tell them that, we kind of cover our backs, so to speak in a sense, otherwise we get into like hazy, murky waters, and what one tutor may accept, another tutor may not accept. Students do compare, we may think they don't, but they actually do.
> *S.*   So, how would you, [ask her to reference] if she had an oral source, which this is clearly?
> *L.*   I would say steer away from oral sources and concentrate on hard, substantial, documented evidence.

So Lyn's advice to students is to reference everything, but when they come up with examples from the media or their lecture notes, and reference them, she does not see this as empirical evidence. They are here to read, and should keep other sources of information out of their essays.

However, the task of this particular Social Sciences discipline in relation to the world that students come from is a particularly difficult one. Many students come to the discipline highly politicized, with particular tools of analysis engendered in the resistance structures of the apartheid era. Lecturers struggle to inculcate new ways of seeing, new academic tools of analysis in these students. It seems that disciplining students to refer to the readings of the field in their writing is one way of bringing students into an academic world, and this can be at the cost of their authority. (One lecturer, during a workshop on referencing, remarked that referencing could be used to bring a student who 'smacks of rectitude' into line.) S1 reflects on this problem with insight:

> *S1.*   I think that we need to rethink referencing across the board, because we are encountering students and we need to be sensitive to these students and offer them the space in fact, to go out and write their thoughts, their thinking on a particular issue, we almost doubt the

capacity of students these days to think independently, in fact there is almost a conspiracy against students that they have the capacity to think, and this may stem from questions of language, it may be purely racist, I don't know. I suspect it's a whole lot of things. I think it's a degree, obviously, of intellectual elitism, as well. . . . They come in far more confident into this university, than the 5 or 6 weeks afterwards, they come in helluva confident, they come in very sanguine about what they're doing, they come in with ideas. Okay, it's a whole lot of things, but I would suspect that if you asked students to write, if you like, a political biography or autobiography in week 1, it would be far more rich, unique, significant, really significant, profound, than if we asked them to do the same exercise in the third or fourth quarter. I think that we actually start to numb them intellectually.

S.   So what has referencing got to do with that?

S1.   Referencing, what we do is we take their authority away, I think. We devalidate them, we say to them, hold on, there are real authorities out there and you need to come to grips with, there are great thinkers, there are profound thinkers, there are thinkers who are better than you, there are more intelligent creatures out there, and what you've got to do, is you've got to engage with these great thinkers and learn from them . . . but implicitly, we are saying, you don't qualify as a thinker, you don't qualify as an intellect, you don't qualify as somebody whom we really take seriously, I mean until you've engaged with the lights of the discipline.

The difficult problem, and one which would not seem important to some of the staff, seems to be how to nurture the authority that some students come with, whilst apprenticing them to the discourse of the discipline and the academy. Part of the difficulty of this discipline is that many of the black students have experienced the oppression of the old South African political system in a way that most of their lecturers have only theorized about. They feel they know it with a depth of understanding that for other groups is not possible. It is my sense that whilst all learning involves disequilibrium, a stripping away of the old authorities, the academy needs to allow space for a reaching back into the old, for the use of prior discourses as resources for the learner and for enrichment of the discourses of the academy. So the first impact of the practice of referencing, or rather an obsession with this practice, and with the policing of plagiarism, is that students' other sources of knowledge are shut out. The student's own authority is reined in, stripped down. Some of this seems to be a necessary process in learning new ways of learning, but some of it seems a shutting out of student's own means of making sense of new knowledge, as well as anything that is not part of the Western canon. Pennycook (1994) has a forthright view on this:

We need to consider the power relationships of academic institutions and the ways in which disciplinary knowledge is as much exclusionary as it is inclusionary.... students become aware that they are not really being encouraged to display their own knowledge or write with originality, but rather are being required to regurgitate set canons of academic knowledge 'in their own words'. In this context, plagiarism might then be seen as a justifiably cynical form of resistance. Alternatively, it might be a sign of giving up in the struggle to claim an academic voice...

(281–2)

Another alarming conclusion that must be drawn is that where a student does take the initiative and use outside sources, she/he is in danger of being accused of plagiarism. This in fact happened to Tshediso in another department, Department P, where he had used a source he had known from his previous studies with UNISA to develop a definition, had duly referenced the source, but was suspected of plagiarism when in fact it was his own work. How a lecturer picks up plagiarism is a delicate business requiring experience and judgement, and needing a considered, consistent response. S1 describes this process, and illustrates using Mangaliso's essay (extract below). Mangaliso's essay was given 0, and handed back to him with the comment, 'I believe this to be extensive plagiarism. I invite you to demonstrate to me that I'm wrong.' In the reproduction of the extract below, and all the assignment extracts following, I have retained original spelling, punctuation and grammar, and reproduced the marker's comments on the essays.

Economic liberalism is the use of the market for carrying out three major tasks of an economy – investment, production and distribution. The Market is a decentralized system. Unlike the edict economy a market economy has many independent centers of decision – Firms that produce goods and services and individuals who consume them. But each operates according to certain rules. And all these rules involve the assertion of maximal self-interest, defined as profit. The market has the virtues of harmony and efficiency. The market has been called a 'system of perfect liberty.' Private ownership is well grounded in liberal states.

Relevance?

Conversely, economic liberalism nurtures political freedom. In theory it is possible for a society whose economy is run by edict to grant its citizens a full panoply of political rights. In practice this is unlikely. The governments of such societies have immense authority. The power to plan and supervise all economic activity is enormous, and it would be deficult to deny to a government vested with such power, broad authority over political life as well.

S. ... what it was about the essay, that made you think that it was plagiarized?

S1. Well, starting with the second page, is that we see certain material that doesn't come out of our course, okay, that's the first thing that I start to see, it's stuff that we haven't covered. So I start to say, okay, maybe the student is doing Economics, there is a book that deals with the economic dimension of Liberalism.

S. Is that something that happens quite often?

S1. More than not.

S. Would you say that students are deliberately drawing on things from other, not only drawing on, plagiarizing from other courses, from their readings, because they know that you don't have access to that.

S1. I've seen it. I've seen it and I've noticed it. [Reads through essay.] Right there are some constructions here which are, they give glimpses of quite sophisticated authority.

S. Such as?

S1. Let's have a look. And in the middle of this paragraph, Economic Liberalism. Now Economic Liberalism is a term that you use in one particular book that I know was recommended by other tutors, and it's one which was not recommended in mainstream of the course that was taken ... Now if you look at things like 'all these rules, all these rules involve the assertion of maximum self interest, defined as profit. The market has the virtues of harmony and efficiency, the market has been called a system of perfect liberty. Private ownership is well grounded in liberal states', now true true, and this is probably about as good as you get in terms of synthesizing, sorry the words, the constructions are used are probably, it is regarded as being the sort of stuff you would expect to see in a textbook anyway. It is pretty sophisticated, it assumes an awful lot and the connection between Economic Liberalism and Political Liberalism is a very sophisticated one. It is clear, but it is still sophisticated. So I sort of notice things popping out at me, saying wow, this is sophisticated, this is a student I didn't have in the first semester, I picked this student up in the second semester, along the way, so I'm not entirely sure about this student anyway.

There are several things of note about this interview extract. S1 is describing a careful process of judgement, echoed by other lecturers and tutors, which takes place when deciding whether a student is plagiarizing. Key factors which are taken into account are sophistication of language and sophistication of ideas. The marker uses his or her knowledge about the student to make judgements about the appropriate level of sophistication for this student. The conclusions at which the marker arrives may be fairly accurate, however, there are several possibilities that are not taken into account. The student's written language may be more sophisticated than their spoken language displayed in tutorials; the student may simply be reserved during tutorials but have fairly sophisticated ideas; if the marker does not know the book concerned, and does not check up on it, then it is possible that the student is paraphrasing and not plagiarizing; the student may be working with someone else whose English is better, or whose mother tongue is English, and using them as a language editor, a process which might be pedagogically useful. In addition, the marker is immediately suspicious of any ideas which are not covered in the course ('we see certain material that doesn't come out of our course, okay, that's the first thing that I start to see, it's stuff that we haven't covered.'). So when Tshediso concludes that the only way around this problem is to stick to the prescribed readings, he has a valid point.

The issue that concerns me is that students writing in a language that is not their first are more vulnerable to false assumptions about the kind of language that they are capable of, and perhaps also the kinds of ideas they are expected to produce. The slide into racist assumptions, for which students (understandably) have sensitive antennae, is an easy shift, as S1 has noted. Pennycook (1994) points out this danger in the context of Hong Kong:

> Plagiarism may also be viewed as a result of the unclear relationship between originality in thought and originality in words in the academic domain. We need to be very cautious here of acting prejudicially against students, especially students who are not writing in their first language, because we assume their knowledge and linguistic skills are not sufficient to have produced a particular idea or phrase.

> (282)

Tshediso, for example, is not the ordinary first-year student: he is a mature student, quite articulate in his second language, who had used English in prison so that his warders and fellow-prisoners would 'feel the weight' of his educated status. Tshediso had been successful in his UNISA studies, and had used English in all his correspondence from prison, was involved in political structures, and knowledgeable about international events in the media. These are the kinds of factors that were not taken into account when making judgements about sophistication in language and ideas, particularly in his essay for Department P, mentioned above, where he was suspected of plagiarism because of the sophistication of his definition of sexual harassment which the essay required students to develop, and for which he had made use of a legal source known to him through his UNISA studies. In order to further demonstrate these problematic assumptions, I have extracted a section from Tshediso's second essay for Department S:

However it is by means of party presentation that the people can effect a permanent change in the political arena, voice their grievances, question or forward proposals, nature of the policies, the method and leaders of the temporary majority parties. This way, a situation of give and take is created, with the parliament being the area of that process. Karl Marx also acknowledges power of the civil society in the effectiveness of the parties.//In Brazil and Argentina, the trade unions who were subordinate to the state despite their enormous influence, had to hand it to the parties to negotiate on their behalf. In Uroguay it was the parties who paved the way to democracy by negotiating with the regime. It is when democracy is in place that the parties have to show their commitment to the ideology, in their choice of whether they shall be transparent and always be with the people and reconcile with their aspirations . . .

reference? This is an important part of civil society

I discussed this part of the essay with his tutor, Claire, after I had told her a little of Tshediso's history, about which she had seemed surprised, and the following interchange occurred:

S. I was wondering about why you asked for a reference here.
C. Okay. Ja, maybe that actually wasn't necessary, I think, perhaps I'd asked for a reference, because he'd said Karl Marx, he hadn't said Marxist thought, or something, and I might have been wanting to know where . . .
S. Oh, so it wasn't a reference for the Brazil and Argentina examples [that you wanted] . . .
C. No, because I would have put that at the end.
S. Okay.
C. I would have put it there, or maybe there.
S. Ja, okay, so you wouldn't have wanted him to reference his example?
C. Ja, but again, I mean that's common knowledge too, so.
S. It's tricky.
C. Maybe I wasn't giving him enough credit, because I suppose at first-year level, and with his first essay, I didn't realize how, you know, what the level of his political knowledge was and I may have not, maybe I didn't give him the benefit of the doubt, maybe I was thinking it was not common knowledge to him.

The remark 'maybe I was thinking it was not common knowledge to him' sums up, I think, the problematic nature of such assumptions in a university which is trying to integrate students from vastly different educational and cultural backgrounds. Apart from an awareness of such assumptions, appropriate policies for dealing with such instances, of course, can be developed. In fact what the marker in Mangaliso's case (S1) did was to leave the way open for his assumptions to be shown to be incorrect: he asked Mangaliso to demonstrate to him that he had not plagiarized. In fact Mangaliso took up this invitation, and had his mark raised to 55%, after he explained that he had thought that if he acknowledged the authors in the bibliography, then he would not be plagiarizing. The irony here, is that I suspected in the interview with him that Mangaliso, in his need to impress, had in fact knowingly reproduced the words of others without acknowledgement. However, this same marker did not give another student, Nothando, the benefit of the doubt.

Nothando is a first-year student whose primary school education in the Eastern Cape consisted of moving from township to rural schools and back to avoid boycotts in schools. She is studying mainly commercial subjects, and discipline S is her only subject with extensive writing. Her other subjects are Statistics, Economics, and Accounting. She passed all these subjects well in June, and for Statistics achieved 90%. (There is no June exam in Department S, and in this subject she had only written the one essay with which this research is concerned.) She had not been required to enrol for English for Academic Purposes, because she had written the Proficiency Test in English for Educational Purposes (PTEEP), and achieved a mark high enough for her to be perceived as not 'at risk'. She is clearly a talented student, conscientious enough to be attending supplementary tutorials in two subjects, yet in terms of developing writing skills she is falling through the cracks of the system, mainly because, I think, she did not do the EAP course in which the writing process is emphasized.

Nothando's essay has large chunks taken from the key text for this part of the course. At this point I would simply like to comment on the response which she received from the same person who marked Mangaliso's essay. He also gave her 0, and wrote, 'This is plagiarism, please read the handbook.' Nothando was not given the benefit of the doubt: she told me that she was mortified by this comment ('I was so embarrassed I was so weak'), and did not have the courage to talk to the marker about the problems in the essay, so her mark remained 0. During the interview with S1, who had marked her essay, he seemed only then to notice the inconsistency in his approach, and says the following:

S1. I'm interested to my own response to this, though, rather that . . .
S.   Yes, I need to ask you that.
S1. I think this, my response to Mangaliso's was more – I can see that I responded to him by acknowledging that he could see, probably, clearly had no conceptual difficulty, and with some order of difficulty that had gone out and tried to find other texts. It took me longer, obviously to identify the problems, and I realized with Mangaliso, that the message to him was that this can be solved quite quickly, but we need to talk about it. Well, with . . . I thought my first response was 'hold on, there's no referencing here, there's nothing here, you're giving me something, you know this is now May, but

you're giving me something and you're saying to me this is an essay, and I'm saying, in my responses, this is not an essay.' And there is kind of an angry dismissive response, 'This is plagiarism, read the handbook', what good is this, you know, who's going to learn from this and clearly, reading the handbook is not good enough for anybody. I think, in a sense, well, gosh how do you explain it, different responses . . . let me look at it more objectively, this is the wrong message.

So S1 is critical of his own response. In thinking through his response, he thinks that he seemed to be giving up on Nothando, dismissing her entirely – her effort was not worth the response given to Mangaliso. In the absence of policy guidelines for markers of essays, it is inevitable that inconsistencies such as these will arise, across markers and within one marker's work. It is neither possible nor pragmatic to check up on all sources used by students. It is possible, here, that issues of gender came into play, and I shall return to this in the concluding chapter.

At this point I would like to contrast the assumptions made above with different kinds of assumptions: where a student is thought to have authority, and is therefore not asked to reference all their sources of knowledge.

Laura is a high-flying first-year student who spent one and a half years at a United World College (UWC) in Singapore, where she received a varied and progressive education which included involvement in international development institutions, youth conferences and so on. She says that writing an essay at the UWC was not too different from what she experiences at UCT. Her tutor, Lyn, showed me Laura's essay because she achieved an exceptionally high mark in her group (95%). Although she has clearly gone out of her way to obtain interesting examples to demonstrate her argument, going so far as quoting from the Court Reporter which she obtained in the Law Library, she does not reference very frequently, and is not asked to. Clearly this student has done more than the required reading, and this is perhaps why she is not always asked to reference. I suspect it has more to do with the assumptions that Lyn is making about this student's authority. The most obvious example of this comes at the end of Laura's essay:

> Francois Mitterand, the now ex-prime minister of France once said to a reporter from the Express, (1993) that it is the established liberal democratic institutions, although necessary, that tend to abuse their power and become oppressive, and it is these that we should fear, liberty is fragile he said, and needs protection, as has become evident in this essay.()conclude therefore by saying that in practice, the institutions of a liberal democracy have fallen short of the expectations of the liberal democratic theory and thus of the public at large. ✓

When I asked Lyn why she generally did not require Laura to reference much, she said:

L.   But as far as I was concerned, it was her first essay, and I obviously knew where this was all coming from. I was just so impressed that she's gone and read this book, I said, jeez, this is wonderful. And in her subsequent essay, she's read Thatcher's book, she's read Kissinger's book for her next essay, I mean, you know and maybe it kind of glazes me over and I don't kind of deal with the nitty gritties well enough.

S.   Well, you probably don't have to. But I want to ask you the same kind of question for this. She actually quotes, fairly closely in detail, without a reference.

L.   The Express, ja. I think that was also leeway allowed by me, which maybe shouldn't have been. Or maybe I wasn't consistent enough. . . . Ja, I don't actually know if she quoted The Express in her bibliography [looks at bibliography] – she didn't.

S.   And in fact she told me that it was a translation, because The Express is French and her mother has these things lying around, and so she translated. I said, 'Which are Mitterand's actual words?' And she said, 'It's a translation', which is also tricky, in terms of what you do with referencing.

L.   I think, in terms of that, I let a lot of it go as general knowledge, which maybe I shouldn't do, just because I don't want to stifle their use of like sources that we wouldn't usually use, or the use of their own knowledge, of general knowledge of politics. A lot of students come to me and say, I didn't do history at school, I don't know general knowledge, which is so wrong, they do, they have so much general knowledge . . .

The question to ask here is whose general knowledge counts? Does Laura's count more than Tshediso's? The words, 'I obviously knew where this was all coming from' are interesting. Though on the surface it is a reference to a knowledge of the sources Laura had used (although in fact she had not known all of them), subconsciously it may be a reference to a shared culture from which Lyn and Laura come. The same tutor who wants 'empirical' (meaning written sources) documentation for all sources, who says students should not use any examples that they cannot find documentation for, has allowed Laura to get away with little referencing, and enthuses here in talking about Laura's essay about how much general knowledge students have, and how she wouldn't want to 'stifle their use of sources that we wouldn't usually use'. Again it may be a question of the establishment of authority in writing in an essay, which Laura is able to do with ease, and which is far more difficult for the second-language learner, or the learner not already steeped in the culture of the academy. To be fair to Lyn, she does not frequently pick students out in her marking for their lack of referencing, although she emphasizes it in the interview with me, and in her tutorials, and she goes so far as to check the references of every sixth essay she reads. What she tells students does not seem to be the same as what she enforces: she seems rather to accept their work as long as it is technically well-referenced and has a reasonable bibliography.

A similar case which illustrates differences in assumptions about particular students is Emma's, the third-year student who obtained a high mark on her essay, and whose essay was not referred to me as having problems with referencing, rather that it was the best essay marked thus far. The following is the first part of Emma's essay:

Extract A

Outline and discuss the explanations for the persistence of civilian rule and/or the emergence of authoritarian regimes, and the emergence of military rule in the Third World.

✓ The 'Third World' for all its political, economic, historical, physical and human diversity, has in common a strong propensity towards military intervention. Military coups have become the 'institutionalised method for changing governments in postcolonial Africa'(Jenkins and Kposowa, 1992: 27). – with the armed forces of Asia, Latin America and the Middle East not far behind when it comes to seizing power. A variety of historians have produced explanations as to why control of the government should so often have been transferred irregularly through the use of force rather than through the democratic pro-

✓ cedures that most Third World states were bequeathed by the departing colonialists, or through the personal choice of the outgoing (usually dying)

NB ✓ civilian dictator. Explanations for the minority of cases where civilian rule persisted, uninterrupted by the military jackboot, seem to rely more on the absence of coup-provoking factors than on any positive factors of civilian regimes.

Foremost among explanations for military intervention is the weakness – the political underdevelopment of the Third World state. In Africa in particular, the European invaders were thrown out (or 'persuaded' to leave) so fast that newly independent countries found themselves with new, rootless, and shaky political institutions in India and parts of the Caribbean, a long period of colonial tutelage led to the formation of an indigenous professional class which monopolised the post-independence leadership and perpetuated civilian, even democratic rule. But in Africa, whatever its rhetoric, the West made no sustained preparation for independence. Often, its actions seemed designed

✓ to prevent any hope of persistent civilian rule – France's eight-year war to 'keep Algeria French'; Portugal's abrupt departure, without even holding elections from Angola, Spain's invitation to Morocco and Mauritania to invade the Western Sahara as it pulled out. Even when workable political institutions were set up, they were 'alien, hierarchical and imposed'.

Extract B

Military rule has emerged in an enormous number of countries, (in the 23 years after 1960, the Third World had over 76 coups) and with an enormous variety of purposes (and pretexts). The simplest explanation is human nature: ✓ virtually everyone thinks they can run the government 'better than the idiots in power – and, as Mao points out, power comes from the barrel of a gun; armies have the ability to turn their dreams into reality. Seizing the banks, ports, radio and TV stations, and government offices is a relatively simple matter (transforming the country – or just ruling it – is another matter, but military rule usually begins with even more ludicrously optimistic hopes (at least on the army's part) than democratic rule.) Small countries like Togo and Sierra Leone are especially easy to take over. Personal ambition and the per-   ✓ ceived interests of the army rank high as reasons for the rude interruption of civilian rule: but there are others. Armies can be genuinely revolutionary – as in Egypt, Libya and Iraq, where they overthrew kings and landlords, redistributed land and nationalized industry.

Emma does a number of things which, comparing her feedback to that of other students in the same course, would require referencing. For example she writes, 'a variety of historians' without mentioning any names. She mentions a great number of historical processes, including reference to specific countries, which she does not source at all. She makes assertions, such as 'Virtually everyone thinks they can run the government "better than the idiots in power"', for which she opens but does not close quotation marks, and does not reference what seems in fact to be her assertion. She quotes Mao directly without reference, she quotes statistics (76 coups after 1960) with no reference. Emma obtained 85% for her essay, and, apart from a few comments in other sections of the essay asking for page numbers or references, usually where Emma had made a technical error, there is no comment overall on her referencing, just the remark 'Excellent essay'.

I believe that this student is well known to the marker, and writes with authority. She is clearly knowledgeable, and is not expected to back up her argument in the way that a less authoritative student might be. When I asked the marker, S3, who you will remember related citation to intellectual traditions and debates, to talk about these sections of the essay, we had the following exchange:

S.   And what I was interested in is the fact that you don't actually ask her for many references there.

S3.   No, one reference. I presume I see that as the introduction and I don't tend to be fussy in the introduction.

          . . .

S.   'In the 23 years after 1960, the Third World had over 76 coups', and she didn't reference that.

S3. Okay, that doesn't worry me.

S.   Now why doesn't it worry you?

S3. Okay, because I think it's the kind of generalized information you kind of pick up from anywhere.

S.   Okay, all right.

S3. I mean if it was of such major significance, that we were doing an analysis of coups, you know what I mean, then I might have a different opinion of it, but it's a kind of generalized statement. Half the world is made up of democracy.

S.   Is it not, also, that you know Emma, and you know that she doesn't suck these things out of her thumb? Is it something to do with that?

S3. I don't think so, I'm not sure, if some students wrote that to me, I mean it would be in a context, let's put it this way. If I thought there was a whole lot of unreferenced stuff, by the time I get to 76 coups, I might well, sort of blow my top and sort of say, where the hell is the reference for that. But if it is generally referenced then I'm not going to get upset about that, so I think the context of referencing is probably quite important.

My reading of what S3 is saying, is that as long as there is sufficient referencing here and there, if it is 'generally referenced' she is not going to be too particular about locating knowledge. She does not seem here, or in the way she marked the essay, to be looking for scrupulous accreditation, or evidence of a knowledge of intellectual traditions and how they interact, which she had spoken of in the interview. When it comes to marking, then, all she seems to require is that the student demonstrates coverage of the course readings. S3 is a lecturer who maintains that referencing is 'absolutely central to academic writing', saying, 'how do we debate different ideas, different theories, if we don't know that they're coming out of different contexts?' She is also the only one of my respondents, who in answer to the interview question 'Does a writer with more authority reference more or less?' answered that a writer with more authority references more. However, it seems here, although S3 does not accept this in the interview extract, that Emma has established her authority, in her writing and in the context of the course, and offers the reader what my colleague Rob Moore has called a 'lubricated journey' through her essay, unsnagged by linguistic problems, and is therefore not required to reference all her sources, and is certainly not accused of plagiarism.

By way of contrast to Emma, the following extracts from another third-year student, Veronica's essay provides a different picture. Veronica calls herself Mauritian, although she was born in Malawi to Mauritian parents. She understands patois but doesn't speak it, and speaks some Chichewa. She is doing a degree in Public Administration, having completed A-levels in Malawi. She had no problem initially at university, recalls getting high marks, but now seems to be less successful. Her essay was selected by her tutor,

Rose, with a note to me saying, 'Poor referencing, no location of ideas, no sense of opposing views in a nuanced manner.'

Extract A

However, Dependency theory loses my support where it implies that the people afflicted 'immiseration' have merely accepted this fate. The theory perceives peasants as an amorphous group when they should be perceived as resilient and resourceful in their survival strategies, and in their adaptation to whatever their circumstances dictate.
Fine, but this is only an assertion. You need to substantiate your opinion with theoretical arguments/case study evidence

Extract B

Cotton, according to Daniel Faber was responsible for most of the damage, having a crop prone to attracting pests. Therefore to combat this large amounts of DDT pesticide was used. Larger amounts had to be used as pests became more resistant to it. This toxic chemical was sprayed on fields over unprotected laborers. A consequence of this was that the land, water, air and people of the region were poisoned. These pesticides used were banned from their countries of origin but somehow manifested themselves in 3rd world countries as Commack argues "The priority given to rapid growth has bred a *refs?* relative lack of concern for environmental consequences: the emphasis upon export earnings has prompted the wholesale despoliation of existing natural resources ... and, ironically, the sustained success in achieving sustained *is this* growth has meant that the process of destruction has continued relentlessly, *the case?* on a number of fronts over a considerable amount of time" (Commack, 1993: 289).

The focus is meant to be the causes of dev. Policies. Another important consequence of the "'development' policy of 3rd world countries is 'the increase in the power of the state and it's militarization." (Leftwich, 1988: 187) It is quite a common ocurrence in 3rd world countries that more of the budget *case* expenditure is spent on defence than on welfare, health and education. Per- *study?* haps this can be explained by the fact that they are under constant threat from within as well as externally. This is especially so in areas where political *refs?* culture has been characterized by instability.

My purpose for including these extracts is to show how very different the requirements of this marker are in terms of referencing. Emma and Veronica are doing the same course, but have chosen two different essay options, and have two different markers. Veronica's essay was marked by Rose, an Honours student[1] who herself references almost every sentence when she writes, and says this about her own writing:

R.   Every sentence that I make, unless it's a linking sentence, of ideas, I reference. . . . I think that I would say that in most of my writing there are two different types of sentences, one which reports ideas, perspectives, that sort of thing, and one which makes connections between things that I've already written down, so I may put down a whole lot of things, a perspective, a counter-perspective and then have my own linking sentence which wouldn't be referenced.

Rose might simply be more thorough than S3 in requiring references to sources; however, the messages that Emma and Veronica are getting through their feedback are very different. In addition, Rose's comment 'Fine, but this is only an assertion. You need to substantiate your opinion with theoretical arguments/case study evidence' is the only comment that I saw in all the essays I analysed (18 third-year and 23 first-year) which actually gave a reason why it is necessary to reference at a particular point in an essay.

I think that this data demonstrates the inconsistencies within one marker's work, and across markers of the same essay, regarding the practice of referencing, and in their approaches to plagiarism, and demonstrates some of the negative consequences of an overemphasis on referencing and the monitoring of plagiarism, in terms of the assumptions made. It also shows that a writer with authority is apparently expected to reference less than one who does not have authority. I return to explore the nature of that authority in Chapters 11 and 12. I now move to some of the more positive consequences of the practice of referencing.

Positive consequences

Lambo, immediately when I think of him, I identify with the holistic approach . . .
they're going to see the kind of overall academic picture . . .
I'm able now to adopt a critical stance . . . I must mention my opponent . . .

Here I wish to examine Tshediso's development over the year. From being highly resistant and critical of the practice of referencing, he began to use it far more successfully in his writing, and began to develop confidence in his use of it as a tool. The following extract, from the last interview of the year, describes his view of the process:

> T. Well before I got used to it, what would happen was when I was reading as a preparation for an assignment or an essay, I would read maybe four readings, and then in my mind I would compile them into one whole, to make a coherent and logical argument, and then I write maybe four or eight pages, as one whole thing. So if I had to mention say Leftwich, immediately my logical flow is interrupted, and then I had to continue, mention somebody else.

S. It was probably quite difficult because you had put those aside, and it was all in your mind, and you didn't know quite where anything was coming from?

T. Exactly.

S. And now?

T. I try to incorporate the authors.

S. How do you do that?

T. For example in this last (Department P) essay, for Lambo, immediately when I think of him, I identify with the holistic approach, so immediately when I write about the holistic approach, then I'm bound to mention him, because he's part of it.

Referencing has taught Tshediso to attach names to approaches or concepts, it has taught him a different way of thinking about things, perhaps a different conception of how knowledge is constructed. He has now learnt to locate authors within frameworks of ideas, such as Lambo with the holistic approach; the focus on referencing has helped him to obtain a wider picture of the context within which he writes. His tutor, Claire, reflecting on the role of referencing, says,

C. ... and realizing that the knowledge is all linked together too, but if they are consistent with the footnotes, if they take note, if they actually notice referencing in the articles they're reading, they'll realize that sources that are being quoted there are sources that they have read themselves, and that are perhaps mentioned in other courses that they've done and they're going to see the kind of overall academic picture, not seeing it as such a fragmented thing.

The next extract from S3's interview continues her thinking on referencing as a manifestation of whether the student is conscious of traditions of thought:

S3. I think that what is very hard for people to come to terms with is their way they think about the world comes out of different traditions, okay. . . . There are thought forms, there are constructions, or how you think about the world. . . . And it's about hierarchy, it's about higher and lower, it's about better and worse, it's about constant judgement and ranking. . . . Okay, so one of the things I like students to be conscious of is where do these ideas come from and they can't know where these ideas come from, if they don't reference them. Because if they don't reference them, then they are not able to understand . . . they don't get to distinguish different, well it's not true. . . . It's not their lack of referencing that doesn't allow them to distinguish different arguments. But if they had a consciousness that this is an author, and this is what the author is saying, then when

> they come to another author, and that author is saying something completely different, if they could hold that information in their mind, my view is that they will start developing over time, a structure or pattern of thought, these are a collection of views, they belong to Mills, I mean just take it right down the line, these other views come from a Marxist tradition, this is what they share in common and this is where they are different.
>
> S. So the problem is manifested in the referencing, or the lack of it, rather than that being the problem.
>
> S3. No, I agree with you. It's manifested, and it's part of a training which has to start very early, because, it is for me the essence of Social Science. How do we debate different ideas, different theories, if we don't know that we're coming out of different contexts.

In this view, then, the practice of referencing encourages students to recognize that knowledge and ideas are constructed, that they belong to certain traditions, schools of thought, they are written by authors within a context. What Tshediso is beginning to do, and it seems to be happening through a consciousness of referencing, is placing people and ideas. He is beginning to get glimpses of the 'overall academic picture', and beginning to get a sense of different authors and theories 'coming out of different contexts', he is beginning to identify the intellectual traditions. Tshediso, it seems, has not gained this consciousness through what he has been taught on the course. Part of his awareness comes from thinking about referencing through this research process, and through the journal in which I asked him to write about his difficulties with referencing. Tshediso continues in the interview to reflect on his new approach to writing, and here I think he is particularly insightful about his reading and writing processes:

> S. So what are you doing in your process of writing that's different now, that enables you to reflect which source you're using in your writing? What are you doing now, so that the referencing is no longer intrusive?
>
> T. Oh I think basically it was because when I read, when I was preparing you know, the best method for me to understand the given subject was to be subjective, to be part of it. Now when I reproduce it, then I reproduce it as if it is mine, it is one whole thing.
>
> S. So you tried to become part of it, it became yours. Now what do you do?
>
> T. Now I become subjective, I get involved to understand it, but now if I have to reproduce it, I read it again, and become objective, like a spectator. I'm able now to adopt a critical stance, so I think it is the best thing for me now, because I have in fact now [inaudible] this person says this, so now I'm going to attack his views, so it's easy, I

must mention my opponent, so and so is saying this, so and so is saying this, and then somebody else is saying no this is not proper, it's supposed to be this way, so automatically referencing is dragged in.

S.   So you're saying now that the referencing is enabling you in a way, to be more critical, to stand back?

T.   Ja I would agree with that. (Pause and laughter.) It's maybe because I have developed to that stage. Or maybe I have been in fact *dragged* to that stage, because now I know that what I have to say, in comparison to what I have read, what I've read in fact carries more weight, it carries more weight. What I read carries more weight so I must reference.

I think that Tshediso makes a very useful distinction between the 'subjectivity' and involvement needed to understand what he is reading, and the 'objectivity' required in academic writing. He is learning, understanding, through involvement of himself in the readings. He is finding that because he references, he is better able to stand out of his writing, adopt a 'critical stance'. It is not possible to be critical of ideas if they are 'facts' that belong to all. If they are constructions of particular authors, if the 'opponent' can be mentioned, then they can be set up for 'attack'. Tshediso is finding that he has to 'get involved' to understand the readings, and then withdraw into spectator mode in order to write. This is his particular way of operating which helps him to move into the readings, and out of the writing. He is still resistant, still resentful of the lack of recognition of his independence of ideas: 'I know that what I have to say, in comparison to what I have read, what I've read in fact carries more weight, it carries more weight. What I read carries more weight, so I must reference.' Tshediso is learning the discourses of the academy, and, in so doing, giving up some of the old authoritative discourses of his past. He has accepted that what he reads 'carries more weight' than what he has to say, and there are gains and losses, which are discussed in Chapter 5, using Kress's theory of 'harmonization' of discourses, in that acceptance of his own lack of authority, for the purposes of success in the academy.

The data suggests, then, that the consequences of the requirement of referencing and the monitoring of plagiarism are both negative and positive. The absence of debate, policies and guidelines on the 'hazy, murky waters' that Lyn speaks of lead to a situation where in practice students are left very confused about how to write, how much of their background knowledge or outside reading it is permissible to bring in, and how to do this. Inconsistencies in marking practices with regard to dealing with 'plagiarism', and how much and what kind of feedback is necessary emerge clearly in the data. Also evident is that students who are seen to write with authority are not required to reference as thoroughly. It is apparent, too, that assumptions about that authority or the lack of it are made somewhat problematically, through looking at sophistication of language and sophistication of ideas, and that speakers of English as an additional language are at a disadvantage as far as such assumptions are concerned.

On the positive side, it seems that a sustained focus on referencing, as occurred through the research process with Tshediso, can lead to a new understanding of the construction of knowledge, and can move the learner from a position of seeing knowledge as an indeterminate mass of information, to a position where he or she is able to locate authors within debates, and throw one perspective up against another in a critical manner.

I move on in the next chapter to the third question, which attempts to explain what may be happening when a student is deemed to have plagiarized by the marker of an essay.

Note

1. In South Africa, the normal social sciences degree takes three years. An Honours student is doing a fourth year of study in one particular discipline and is considered a postgraduate.

10

Plagiarism in the developing writer – what's really happening?

This chapter investigates some of the reasons why first-year students 'plagiarize', or are thought to be plagiarizing, and relates to some of the categories discussed theoretically in Chapter 5. I do not deal here with the frequently reported misconception that if the writer acknowledges something in the bibliography, then they do not need to reference in the text. Moreover, I concentrate on the 'word-for-word' form of plagiarism, rather than plagiarism of ideas, as the latter is very difficult to enforce (as its omission from copyright law indicates). Tshediso highlights the problem for the first-year student when he says,

> *T.* ... Before coming to UCT, I knew nothing of what liberal democracy is. So whatever I know, I got it from the lectures and maybe from Cartwright.[1] Now if I'm asked to discuss liberal democracy, now whose work is it? If I'm going to use Cartwright do I after each and every sentence say 'Cartwright' and then write another sentence? ... So just randomly I put 'Cartwright'.

In other words, Tshediso is saying that everything he knows about liberal democracy comes from what he has learnt in his first-year course, which implies that each sentence would need to be referenced. It seems too that most markers, though they understand plagiarism to include the use of the ideas of others without acknowledgement, are generally fairly lenient when this occurs in student essays. They are annoyed far more by word-for-word copying, whether acknowledged or not. This is thus my area of focus in this section.

'Trying on' the discourse

You take a book and read it, and . . . you get some skills of writing.

Bulelwa matriculated in a small village in the Eastern Cape, which she had never left until she came to UCT. She wants to do a degree in Public Administration. She had very little conversation in English at school; she only really heard English in the Maths class (because her teacher was Ghanaian) and the English class. She described English at her school as 'not a very medium language' because the teacher 'often turns the language to the Xhosa language'. She studied the Bible by correspondence for three years, posting off assignments to King William's Town, and getting responses. She also spent two years after school as a part-time secretary for an irrigation scheme, where she had to do work requiring basic literacy skills, such as marking absentees, accounting for crops of cabbages, and so on. She still reads the Bible regularly, and goes to church, but besides this has no other activities at UCT as 'it's too difficult to cope with my work, so I neglected everything'. She is now talking more English because she shares a room in residence with a Tswana-speaking woman, so they communicate in English. When I telephoned Bulelwa to ask her to come for an interview, she did not seem to understand me; when I said I wanted to talk about her essay, she thought I wanted her to write an essay in my office. I later approached her through the EAP lecturer who taught her on the EAP course. She seemed fairly relaxed during the interview, although it was sometimes obvious that expressing herself in English required effort and concentration.

Towards the end of the year, Bulelwa was still producing essays which were perilously close to the sources: her EAP lecturer showed me her first draft of her final EAP essay, where the tutor had written, 'The essay has total plagiarism, i.e. you write straight from the article, and do not alter words.' The following is an extract from her interview, where she is talking about the role of referencing.

S.   Anything else? Why we reference?
B.   Okay I mean tutors want to see the, want to develop your skills in, by by looking to someone's work.
S.   Yes – how do you mean?
B.   I mean . . .
S.   They want to develop your skills . . .
B.   By by looking to someone's work in a way that you take a book and and read it, and then you, you get some skills of writing. Of collecting, of collecting your information, and the, the style.
S.   So by reading, you get writing skills, is that what you're saying?
B.   Yes.

S.   Explain to me a little bit more about that? If you read an article, what are you learning about writing skills?

B.   Okay, you, you learn what must come first, and then what comes first and then, and and and the the information which is not useful, you can see that from from the style of an author.

S.   Okay so from reading, you're gaining information, or skills about writing in terms of what must come first, what information is not useful, and so on. What else are you learning?

B.   Oh, from the reading?

S.   Mmm. It's interesting what you say, I'm just interested in what you're saying, because you're saying that actually from the reading you're learning something about how to write yourself. Anything else there that you feel you're learning from reading? You said something about style. What do you mean by style?

B.   The way he describes things.

S.   Yes? For instance? (Silence) The way an author describes things? (Silence) You mean the words that they use?

B.   Mm, the words that they use.

It seems to me that Bulelwa, difficult as it is for her to articulate it, is using the text that she reads as a very necessary learning scaffold, to help her to write. She is modelling her writing on what she reads in terms of structure ('what comes first'); selection of important information ('the information which is not useful', although how the text can help one to discard information in the text itself which is 'not useful' is not clear); and the 'way the author describes things', which seems to mean the actual words used. She also seems to be using 'EAP-speak', language about writing which she has picked up on the English for Academic Purposes course.[2] Bulelwa needs to step into the shoes of the author in order to write.

Legitimate language, understandings of knowledge construction, and the role of formulaic language

sometimes it loses its sense when I use his words ...

Consociationism, I would prefer them to call it power-sharing.

A later discussion on Bulelwa's reading and note-taking process confirms her dependency on the text, and emphasizes her lack of confidence in her own language, the feeling that her own understanding is far inferior to that of the authority, the text itself:

S.   Okay, so you take notes using the words of the author, and when you're writing you paraphrase?

B. Yes.

S. Why do you do that?

B. When I'm taking notes? Ja I, I want to understand what was he saying.

S. And you feel that if you put it in your own words – ?

B. If I wanted to – okay I can say I, I, by paraphrasing it I don't want to to plagiarize.

   . . . By using words, his words, I mean I lose lots of marks because sometimes I usually forget to write his name and then sometimes it it loses its sense, when I use his words. I mean the sense of what I'm trying to explain.

S. It loses its sense when you use *his* words? How do you mean?

B. Let's say, as I've taken the notes, ne? I paraphrase most of this. So if I want something to be clearer, sometimes I use his words sometimes I use mine. So that I mean by that I'm trying to, it depends the way I've explained it.

S. So you feel that if you use somebody else's words sometimes, it's clearer?

B. Yes sometimes – it depends what I'm saying.

This interview probably would have revealed far more if it had been conducted in Xhosa, but I shall do my best within the constraints of her difficulties with English to interpret her words. This rather confusing discussion nevertheless reconstructs Bulelwa's reasons for using the writer's words when she takes notes, in an intriguing way. Initially she is quite clear: she wants to 'understand what was he saying', and so she takes notes using the author's words. She is implying that if she puts it in her own words, then when she goes back to those notes, she will not understand what the author was originally getting at: she does not trust her own interpretation, her own paraphrase of the original. When writing, she paraphrases, so that she will not be plagiarizing ('by paraphrasing it I don't want to plagiarize'), yet she realizes that 'sometimes I use his words, sometimes I use mine', and that if it is in somebody else's words it is sometimes clearer. This is not a matter of trying to impress by sophisticated language, as in Mangaliso's case, it is simply a matter of a lack of confidence in the adequacy and legitimacy of her own means of expression in writing, and in her own understanding of the original text.

   Sherman (1992) found in discussions with her plagiarizing Italian students that they too considered it disrespectful to presume to re-express the words of an expert, and she compares her students' difficulties to extracting corks from bottles:

On the one hand the corks they are dealing with, the texts and other sources, are to their perception solid intractable lumps which must be treated with respect – and this means preserving their integrity; on the other hand, they do not have the appropriate corkscrew, the dialectical approach, for penetrating the corks and subduing them to their purposes. They may also have some feeling that they are not in any case entitled to open this sort of bottle.

(193)

Bulelwa is aware that her attempts at paraphrase sometimes become plagiarism, and tries to avoid it, but at the same time seems unable to do anything other than use the author's words, mixed with her own. This is further confirmed when we are discussing her actual essay:

S. How close is your paraphrase? How much do you change it, or do you just change a few words?

B. No I used to change the whole, I mean I used to look at synonyms of the words.

S. Yes. That's how you do it, your paraphrase? You look at synonyms? How do you get the synonyms?

B. Some I get from dictionary.

S. So you get some synonyms and then you just put the synonyms in to change it.

B. Mm.

Although she says that she changes the whole (and this is probably a defensive answer to a question that might have seemed accusatory), she then says that the way she does it is to look up synonyms in the dictionary. This must be a tedious, time-consuming process which she cannot sustain throughout a long essay. Through the use of synonyms then, she is changing some of the lexicon, but probably little of the syntax of sentences, and thus the language used is still very close to the original. This is where the writer of English as a second or third language is at a substantial disadvantage: the elegant paraphrase is beyond their reach, and very difficult to sustain through an eight-page piece of writing.

Lindiwe, the student who over-references 'to attract the marker', has a different strategy, but with similar underlying reasons. She manages to avoid being accused of plagiarism, by (usually) acknowledging the authors, but some of her paragraphs consist almost entirely of a (referenced) quotation from a reading. The following extract from her essay illustrates a quotation side by side with what seems to be a very close paraphrase, or the author's exact words, which represents the entire paragraph:

Now democracy and liberal are combined together to form Liberal Democracy. These are not too different concepts as they both has to do with freedom but in democracy freedom has to be in some certain extent. 'For Lenin Democracy is a form of the state one of its varieties . . . The libereral state is the dictartorship of the bourgeoisie, but because of its democracy representative character it signifies the formal recognition of equality of citizens' (Duncan∧ 1983: 88) ✓

It thus points to a future in which the ideals associated with democracy could be manifested through the removal of restrictions that the wider social context imposed. (Duncan∧ 1983: 88)

Lindiwe is talking about the reasons for her use of long quotations from Duncan, shown above, in the extract below:

L.   Another thing, for me I think it's it's very difficult like to put some-thing in my own words. I find it difficult.
S.   Why?
L.   Because sometimes I felt that if I put it in my own words then it's not going to give the same meaning as the author's. I've found that.
S.   Mm. So you're afraid you might distort the meaning if you put it into your own words?
L.   Mm.
S.   Okay right so in the last paragraph when you write Duncan there – ja the bottom paragraph, would you say these are Duncan's words or your words?
L.   I think I omitted some of the words.

It seems that Lindiwe has a similar underlying problem to that of Bulelwa: she is afraid that if she uses her own words when writing (Bulelwa when note-taking) she will not represent the author's meaning clearly enough. Bulelwa writes notes which contain the author's original words, and then transfers them with a few synonyms into her essay. Lindiwe simply takes large chunks of the author's original words, and places them in her essay in quotation marks. She talks in other parts of the interview of the words of the author being well-written and 'clear to understand'. Because the words of the authorities 'cannot be represented, only transmitted', as Bakhtin (1981: 344) writes (see Chapter 5 for discussion), Lindiwe uses them directly and does not try to (or cannot) interpret them or work with them in any way. When she does not quote directly, then she 'omitted some of the words' – her paraphrase simply leaves out some of the words of the original. It is also clear that Lindiwe's conceptual distance from the texts she reads is vast. Describing the difficulty she has in working with sources, she says:

S.   Now when you've been writing essays have you found referencing easy or difficult?
L.   It's difficult. It's difficult because sometimes like you like sometimes you you found something in that particular book, ne? then you don't know like how to summarize like sometimes like a paragraph, you don't know how to like make it short, and to, you don't know which

part are you going to leave and which are you going to put in, and you don't know how to reference that particular thing.

S. Okay – just explain to me a bit more. So you find, if you find a passage in a book, you don't know how to condense it.

L. Ja to make it short.

S. So what do you do then?

L. Sometimes you think of putting the first sentence in, you don't think about what about the following sentences, maybe they are more important than the first one you are putting in.

It seems that Lindiwe has no way of knowing what is important in what she is taking from the texts. She does not know how to summarize, or select ('you don't know which part are you going to leave and which are you going to put in') so she simply puts in the first sentence which seems remotely relevant. Elsewhere in the interview, when I ask her how she found the readings, she replies:

L. They were also difficult because maybe you read this reading and compare this to the other ones – I find it difficult to compare, between both readings. How am I going to take this and leave this out . . . the other thing that is difficult is the terms used in the readings. Every time I see this term I've got to go to the dictionary and look, it takes time.

So here Lindiwe seems to be expressing a difficulty in comprehending the texts she reads, in terms of the lexicon used, in terms of selection of relevant information, and particularly in comparing readings (she mentioned the difficulty of comparing readings several times in the interview). Selection, summarization and comparison are difficult skills, requiring a high order of comprehension. Lindiwe's difficulty also seems to be in seeing texts as the constructions of authors, which can be compared and debated. She sees them as sources of facts and information, and therefore it is difficult to compare: two authors may be presenting the same set of facts, or completely different sets of facts. A sense of texts as presenting perspectives or arguments, which can be critically weighed up against one another, is missing. Nothando reveals a similar problem when she says:

N. So like I have to go to – there are a variety of textbooks to go to, and they are sort of talking about the same thing, but they are, their titles are not the same, but . . . in them there is the same information.

S. This is in [Department S]?

N. Ja. There is the same information, but – I find it difficult to – (Pause)

S. It's difficult to express yourself? (Pause) Okay so you're saying that if you go to the [Department S] courses, there's a variety of textbooks with the same information, but – what's the but?

> *N.* But there are articles – their topics they are not the same, like you go to International Affairs, and International Politics say, International Relations, but inside the textbook there is the same information, like you see that they are talking about nearly the same things.
>
> *S.* So what you're saying you're struggling with is, let's try to clarify this, there are textbooks where the titles are not the same but inside there's similar information, so why is that confusing or difficult?
>
> *N.* I find that in my essay I'm sort of repeating the same things, like I have to go to various textbooks, now when I'm writing I'm sort of repeating the things so I couldn't reach the length of the essay.
>
> *S.* So you haven't found all that much information.
>
> *N.* Because everything is the same.

Nothando is not detecting or looking for authorial stance, perspective or argument in the texts she reads. It is unlikely that all the texts she reads are 'talking about nearly the same things', but as she seems to be looking for facts, not arguments or perspectives, then to her it seems the same.

To return to the problem of comprehension of readings, it seems that the minimum requirement for lecturers when marking a student essay are signals that the student has understood what they have read, and these signals may be found in the nature of the paraphrase, and in whether a student is able to illustrate by example. When I asked them how close a paraphrase is acceptable in an essay, S1 and S2 had similar answers:

> *S1.* Well, I mean, it changes, and our expectations change, obviously, from first year onwards, but at the minimum, Shelley, I think that I look for, or the one technique that I recognize and understand is when a student, at the minimum, can step outside of the material, and illustrate by example, give an example of what the author is saying. If they're unable at that point to paraphrase excessively, I want them to be able to illustrate to me that they understand what that general point means by illustration. So, it's a way, so the minimum I look for is that ... There is a general point of looking for, do you understand this material, I mean is there an understanding there, can you take this material and work with it and can you make the connections? What you're left with, with a sort of cut and paste, is this uncertainty, of not knowing whether the student has understood the material, that's the problem. In a sense, we're asking for the students to demonstrate that understanding.

So for S1 it is important that there is some demonstration of understanding, and the one that he finds most telling is whether the student is able to illustrate by example. This is an interesting point, seeing that tutors sometimes do not want students to draw examples from their own knowledge, but rather expect them to reference whatever examples they use. So the tutor, in insisting on rigorous referencing, is making it difficult for the student to demonstrate understanding through illustration, though of course it is possible, if the student has a written, referenceable source at hand. S2 also looks for understanding:

S.   How close a paraphrase is acceptable?

S2.   That is an extraordinarily difficult question, it is a matter of judgement. The criterion I would be interested in is essentially, is this student showing evidence of having understood what is said or are they merely parroting? . . . You find it in the context and usually the parroters will give themselves away because they paraphrase parts of the chapter or book, whatever it may be, which actually doesn't have very much to do with the argument they're making. Whereas, if it clearly fits in precisely as part of a continuous and cogent argument, then I would take the view they've understood. But, as I say, it is a matter of judgement and I'm sure I make mistakes, I mean, we're not dealing with an exact science here, as you know. And even if we were, it is not a science that we have the resources to practice.

In contrast, Lyn, the tutor who emphasizes referencing, when asked about paraphrase, has this to say:

L.   Obviously, it cannot be word for word, also, if the words kind of got long and odious, and he used quite sort of theoretical terminology, I don't actually know how to phrase this, and I would prefer it, for example, if you talked about, consociationism, I would prefer them to call it power-sharing.

S.   Okay. What is that word you used?

L.   Consociationism, it is kind of a model, which is basically power-sharing, I'd rather that they found their own words, not for every single word, that would be unreasonable and it would be really stupid, but if they wrote three or four sentences, well, let's put it like this, if they wrote two sentences, straight from Cartwright, I would have a problem with that. One sentence? – I don't know, there is a fine line. I would maybe indicate under the paragraph, and maybe say to them, try to use more of your own language or vocabulary, or something like that. Also, it makes more sense for them, it would be easier for them, in terms of argumentation to deal with it, if they know what they're talking about.

It is interesting that Lyn talks about theoretical terminology, and picks a discipline-specific word to illustrate her point. It seems to me that theoretical terms, words which have particular meanings within particular disciplinary contexts, and are known in those contexts, are particularly difficult to substitute; even if one finds the word in a dictionary, it may not be used in the same way in the literature of the discipline. If a student comes across such a word in a reading, and it is not explained to them, and if there is no equivalent word to be found in a dictionary, then the safest would be to use that particular word. The student may guess that it means something close to power-sharing, but it may have a more specific meaning, and therefore it would be more appropriate to retain that particular word. Also, perhaps this particular word is one amongst many that the student is encountering which is entirely new. She is learning that word as part of a semantic field, and may reproduce it formulaically, within a chunk of words, perhaps, as part of her learning the discourse of Department S, as well as the English language.

Overall, it seems that the lecturers I interviewed are fairly tolerant of some word-for-word rendition at first-year level, as long as there is some understanding demonstrated. Tutors seem to be a little less tolerant, perhaps because the experience and judgement called for in evaluating comprehension, referred to by S1 and S2, is lacking.

Hybridization of discourses

As discussed in Chapter 5, I use Bakhtin's term 'hybridization' to describe the contestation between different discourses, past and new, as represented in student writing. For the reader's interest I have included in Appendix 1 a brief analysis and explanation of the writing which students had done in their prior education, in order to demonstrate that the kind of writing that students are encountering at university is generally entirely new. I make no claims as to the generalizability of these tables; however, some distinct patterns emerged, which I think are significant.

It is clear that the students whom I interviewed had very little previous experience in writing from multiple sources. Their dominant experience was in descriptive or narrative composition (called 'creative' writing in the tables), and where 'factual' writing was required, it seemed to be simply a matter of composing from one source, the textbook. Only those who achieved high marks in their essays (Emma and Laura) reported any experience of writing from multiple sources, with the exception of Mangaliso. I think that it follows logically from these prior educational experiences in writing, that students will encounter enormous difficulty in the genres of the academic essay, where they are expected to integrate multiple sources, and, underlying that, to have some understanding of knowledge as constructed, with multiple viewpoints and perspectives being possible.

In addition to this, several of the black students interviewed mentioned their religious experience: Nothando had been the secretary of her Youth

Guild for two years, Bulelwa studied the Bible by correspondence for three years, still reads it regularly, and attends church. Busisiwe was also the Youth Secretary for her church. Mangaliso, too, was a regular churchgoer. I mention this because I would like to suggest that the study of and respect for religious texts, such as the Bible or the Koran, reinforced by the notion of the school textbook as authority, may lead to a particularly entrenched notion of the text as fact, which may conflict fundamentally with the academic essay, where texts are to be compared and contrasted, discussed and challenged, criticized and evaluated.

To summarize then, the skill of referencing rests on an underlying ability to synthesize multiple sources into a coherent whole. The problem of plagiarism may arise from a situation where the student learning a new discourse is unable to do anything other than use the words of the texts she is reading in her writing, as a way of 'trying on' the discourse. It may arise where the student's lack of confidence in her reading and her ability to paraphrase leads to an overdependence on text. The reproduction of discipline-specific terms may be appropriate, and the reproduction of chunks of language that the learner has stored in her memory may be evidence of a normal language learning process, rather than plagiarism. Underlying 'plagiarism' may also be the experience of the text as a set of facts, or as authoritative Book to be respected through faithful imitation.

The final question examines the nature of authorial voice, and how students struggle with placing themselves in their writing, when using multiple texts.

Notes

1. A prescribed book for this course; the author's name has been changed here.
2. I am grateful to Lucia Thesen, who teaches on the EAP course, and who read a draft of this chapter, for pointing this out to me.

11

Developing authorial voice using multiple sources – difficulties and successes

If Giddens is talking about another author, maybe that author is Marx, so I dunno which one to put in, so I just put Giddens . . .

I must present a dead paper now.

My argument hinged on good referencing – it showed that many people were on this side.

I could be able to write a lively paper that I'll be proud and satisfied with which would include referencing . . .

In this section I would like to explore some of the difficulties inherent in the development of an authorial voice in academic writing, some of the hindrances that students experience, in particular how the use of sources and feedback on referencing can inhibit this development in important ways. Detecting the voice of the author when reading a text, which itself is using multiple sources, is as challenging as constructing one's essay in such a way that one's own authorial voice comes through. Sensitivity to authorial voice, detecting authorial stance, is difficult for any reader who does not know the context of writing, and in particular does not fully control the language they are reading, because shifts in authorial stance may be very subtle, indicated by Goffman's (1974, in Scollon, 1995) laminator verbs, as discussed in Chapter 5, or other subtle constructions. The problem that students experience in reading in this regard may manifest itself in their writing. Tshediso's first essay shows clear evidence of this:

Liberal democratic practices diverge from those specified in its theory. In 'Democratic Liberalism in South Africa', Dr Welsh (1987) says there is 'evidence of a perverse unwillingness to strip away the veils that hide and mystify the class relations of a developing capitalist system fundamentally oriented to the goal of capital accumulation'.

I would not have picked it up, nor did his own tutor, but the Head Tutor, after a marking workshop in which he had seen Tshediso's essay, explained to me that in the passage which Tshediso had quoted from Welsh, the author was summarizing a revisionist critique of capitalism, behind which Welsh as author did not stand. Tshediso read it and quoted it as Welsh's viewpoint.

Lindiwe talks about this difficulty with regard to referencing in the following way:

L. Sometimes, in a book, ne? like the author is writing about someone else, another author's ideas, then you dunno how to put that in.

S. What would you do if you wanted to do that? I know you say you're finding it difficult, but what would you do?

L. I think I usually write the author who writes the whole book, like saying that if it's Giddens, if Giddens is talking about another author, maybe that author is Marx, so I dunno which one to put in, so I just put Giddens and put the date and page number.

So for Lindiwe and Tshediso the solution is simply to portray an author's discussion of another author as the work of the author they are reading. Lindiwe seems aware of the problem in this, whilst Tshediso did not detect the authorial stance in the Welsh text. Again I think this can be traced to a lack of understanding of the way in which academic texts are constructed on prior texts, how this is indicated through referencing, and the difficulty for the second-language speaker of detecting authorial stance in the writing.

In addition, academic writing often avoids the use of 'I', so that authorial voice may be particularly difficult to detect. 'I would like to argue that' is often replaced by 'It is argued that', for example. For someone who is not familiar with this kind of discourse, *who* is talking here is opaque, especially where other voices are being discussed. Where this is discouraged in academic writing, the task of the student in showing where the voice of another author ends, and their own begins, is made more complicated. Lindiwe's tutor, Lyn, did not like the use of 'I' – I came across many instances in her marking where she had crossed this out, or circled it as she does in Lindiwe's essay reproduced below:

According to the dictionary of modern politics Liberal Democracy is described as something which is what most developed Western nations would claim to practise. ✓ It is stated that it actually a combination of two values which do not necessarily go together logically. As far as the democracy aspects is concerned liberal democracy is a form of representative democracy. ✓ What

(I am trying to show here is that these two concepts that is liberal and democracy are two controversial concepts which can be argued for and against.

Lindiwe talks about this section of her essay:

S. Top of page 3, you've got 'According to the dictionary of modern politics'. Now which part of this paragraph comes from that dictionary?
L. (Reads. Pause.) I think it's from 'liberal democracy' to 'practice'. Then the following sentences I just wrote it myself.
S. Okay and when you say 'it is stated'?
L. Okay, ja I took it from the dictionary, then I put it in my own words.
S. Okay. Um –
L. Another thing that I can't understand is that I said 'As far as' . . . then I said what I'm trying to show, then Lyn commented there, that I shouldn't use 'I'. She did in the tutorial commented about when someone is writing an essay she can't use the first person. I can't get it, I really can't. . . . So what am I supposed to write, like when I want to give my ideas, my own views?

Faced with Lyn's disapproval of 'I', compounded by her difficulty in representing the voice of the dictionary, where she used 'it is stated', Lindiwe does not know how to bring in her own voice, and indicate this for the reader, in contrast with what has gone before. There are ways of doing this without the use of I, but it would certainly make Lindiwe's task easier if 'I' were permitted.

Tshediso struggled with this problem throughout the year. When his first Department S essay was returned to him with the comment, 'Try not to use very descriptive language which is inappropriate in an academic context (but retain originality!)' his confusion is evident in the following discussion:

S. So it's fascinating, because you have a very strong sense of the need for writing to have a soul, and clearly you tried to do that in your essay, to have some 'soul'. Now how does one do that, and be academic?
T. Ja! That's the most difficult thing. Because when I read a comment of the person who marked my paper, and I was advised, I wonder whether it's an advice or a comment, that my language is too descriptive, they said it is too descriptive, for academic purposes, and at the same time, in fact I'm being encouraged to be original. I think that is – it's a contrast.
S. Mm. So what are you going to do about that?
T. To retain originality and yet at the same time discard the methods I use, I think it's going to be very difficult, it's going to be very difficult. Then I might have to write something – I must present a dead paper now. And but if – this is an academic paper, if it is required of me to do so, then I'll make a gallant attempt – to present a dead paper.

So at this stage of his writing development Tshediso seems to feel that there is no way that he can retain some authorial 'life' in his academic writing. However, by the end of the year, when he wrote a Department P essay for which he obtained a mark of 72%, he felt very differently, though he still experienced some problems. He told me that he had realized that referencing was going to be very important in this particular essay, and so had looked through his course reader to see if there was a reading with lots of references that he could use as a model. He did not find one, so he used as a model a paper which I had written, using data from an interview with him, and which I had given to him to read and comment on (Angélil-Carter, 1997). We were discussing an entry to his journal on referencing in the following interview extract:

S. Your entry that says 'I'm beginning to like this referencing because it gives my essay a sophisticated academic touch.' Could you explain how the referencing does that?

T. Okay for example in fact I'll again use the Psychology essay. It's complicated for starters to compile different ideas into one whole. And then out of that you produce an argument, and at the same time you keep on mentioning this person says this and you give the date, this person says this, you give the date, and so on, but at the end they are saying the very same things. It shows that you are using different readings, they did not in fact directly say those things, you have in fact idealized, or extracted from the reading relevant information that is going to agree with what you are saying.

S. And that's you then, coming through.

T. Yes exactly. After writing my essay, reading it through, I was impressed even myself that I've used different readings, four readings, maybe like in one paragraph, putting it into one whole – yeah, it looked very good.

Tshediso is now able to produce an argument, integrating several readings into a coherent whole which supports his argument. He is also aware that in rerepresenting the sources, he is transforming them ('they did not in fact directly say those things, you have in fact idealized, or extracted from the reading relevant information that is going to agree with what you are saying'). I do not believe that he is misrepresenting these sources, he is simply aware of the transformation which occurs in any intertextual rerepresentation. We continued as follows:

S. Why does it look good?

T. That is going to be difficult for me to explain, but I know that it looks good. I'll make an example with your paper that you compiled and then showed to me. I read it several times okay – in the beginning I did not understand it, but now, because I said this is another reading, this is a different reading, and so forth. I first ignored the referencing, and tried to understand the subject, the whole thing, the crux, and then it just sort of fell into place. Now then I read it with the referencing inclusive, and immediately what jumped to mind is 'So these are different readings, completely different readings, but now they've been compiled into one whole thing that makes sense. Okay there is in fact evidence of a difference, like an author might not agree exactly with the next one, but there is a commonality between.' So I think it was a challenge for me ... In fact, at the beginning, when I was preparing for the essay, each and every reading, it was like on its own, it was just on its own, it had a different concept from the others that followed. But now I knew that I had to construct, argue one whole argument out of this, to integrate them. So once I viewed the results, I realized that I'd done it, it had that sophisticated look, like I'm saying, here it's this, so and so is saying this, Lambo is saying this, those were totally different readings, but now they just flowed into one whole thing. . . . But the most important thing is we had lots of readings and we've been told that none of the authors say exactly, I agree with this and this, they're just ordinary readings, and I have to reference, and I knew that if I could master referencing very well, then it would go a long way. So I went over our tutorial reader, to find maybe one single author, who has made many references but who's dealing with one issue, and there were not very many. And then, then I took your paper. Then I went to it and I said okay this is in fact a discussion about one whole thing, but many references, and in some instances you quoted, and I looked at how you, why did you have to quote here, and I went through it over and over, over it again, in fact it took me a week, the last essay took me a week to compile, and after that I knew how to do it. . . . I knew I was going to do well with the referencing, in fact my whole argument depended on good referencing. Because I had to show that so many authors agree with this view, and they are giving examples that this will work, and this way and this way, because if I don't reference my argument – the more I displayed that so many authors agree with this, the better was my argument, to give it more substance. What I mean by saying that my argument hinged on good referencing – it showed that many people were on this side.

I was intrigued by the way that Tshediso had used my article (which was in fact originally completed as an assignment for an M.Ed. course I was taking: it was this 'student' version that Tshediso saw) as a model for his own writing. It brought home to me the fact that what students normally see as models for their own academic writing are a different genre from the academic essay required for curriculum purposes (could it be that the threat of possible plagiarism of essays discourages staff from providing model essays?). It also highlighted the lack of mediation of how to write academic essays, and within that how to integrate and reference multiple sources, other than some feedback on essays, the occasional mention of referencing in tutorials, and the handbook entry. This was further borne out by the fact that none of the third-year students, and certainly none of the first-year students, even those who had referenced well, and only one of the tutors, expressed anything of the understanding of the role of referencing that Tshediso was articulating by the end of the year. I understood, therefore, that the research feedback process, together with the reflection on writing taking place in the interviews and by means of the journal on referencing, had had a powerful impact on Tshediso's learning. In talking about this with Tshediso, at the end of the final interview, we had the following exchange:

S. So it raised your awareness?
T. Exactly, and such was not the case in the beginning. In fact I merely concentrated on the substances of the subject, the content. I did not think referencing was important, I just thought it was one of those requirements one can comply with if one wishes. I did not see any significance in it at all. In fact I perceived it as, it was sort of a hindrance. But now, after talking about it, I began to understand its nature, its significance, the purpose it's supposed to serve, and the most important thing, that it can be done. I never believed for one second that I could be able to write a lively paper that I'll be proud and satisfied with which would include referencing, and I think I've done it with this [Department P] paper.

So Tshediso has moved from feeling that he had to present a soulless, 'dead' essay, to a point where he has found a way of being 'lively' and academic at the same time. He has also begun to understand the 'nature', 'significance' and 'purpose' of referencing.

In the concluding chapter, I attempt to pull together the voices heard in Part II, and discuss the beginnings of a pedagogy for plagiarism and referencing.

Part

III

Conclusion: *a finale*

12

A pedagogy for plagiarism and referencing

In this conclusion I summarize some of the findings of this exploration into plagiarism and the practice of referencing, and attempt to begin to develop a pedagogy for dealing with the problem of plagiarism and the appropriate documentation of sources within the curriculum.

In Chapter 3 I attempted to deconstruct the notion of plagiarism, to uncover it as an ill-defined concept, its definition further obscured by differences in what constitutes plagiarism across genres. Beneath the veils of the concept itself, lie problems which result from the undirected manner in which plagiarism is detected and sanctioned. Mabizela (1994) reports that the students whom he interviewed expressed an unwarranted fear of plagiarism. Mabizela states that plagiarism 'has become a monster to these students' and 'Perhaps warning regarding plagiarism was over-emphasised by the lecturing staff while, on the other hand, they fail to teach students how to acquire the skill of writing an essay/assignment' (34). So also beneath the veils lie the problems of academic literacy, and the following have emerged in relation to problems with referencing: a confusion about the role of referencing, difficulties with comprehension of and reshaping texts, lack of understanding of how knowledge is constructed, the need to imitate in the early stages of learning a new discourse, the academic essay as an unknown and untaught genre of writing, and the complexity of controlling multiple voices within a text while allowing a writer's voice to be heard. These are difficulties experienced by all students. Also evident in relation to plagiarism, particularly where it concerns students using English as an Additional Language, is the fact that all language is learnt and reproduced in chunks or formulas, so that phrases which are reproduced word-for-word, or only slightly altered, may be a necessary part of the language learning process. Compounding the problem for these students is the lack of optional vocabulary and syntax available to them in their additional language when they are attempting to use their own words in paraphrase.

Thus there are a range of underlying causes for plagiarism in student writing, few of which seem to be intention to deceive. I have deliberately not dealt with intentionally fraudulent plagiarism in any way. It is my belief that plagiarism is much more a problem of academic literacy than academic dishonesty, although the latter of course does take place.

Having deconstructed notions of plagiarism in Part I, and raised questions about what occurs around the practice of referencing and the way it is enforced in Part II, my first thesis in this conclusion is that far from being simply technical and peripheral, what one lecturer described as 'a modern bureaucratic fad', the practice of referencing is a fundamental part of academic discourse. *Knowing who said what* is essential to a deep understanding of any discipline, an understanding of knowledge as constructed, debated and contested. My second thesis is that plagiarism should be viewed as primarily a developmental problem. Following from these two arguments is the third: the practice of referencing, and the deeper understandings of knowledge construction that it represents, should be given a serious place in the curriculum. In order for this to happen, the following need to take place:

1. The negotiation of shared meaning around the concept of plagiarism, including an examination of assumptions linked to this concept in its monitoring and enforcement, and emerging from this, the development of written policy and guidelines, both institutional and departmental.

2. The development of an academic literacy programme within the curriculum, which includes a focus on referencing within the academic essay. This means attention to the complexities of developing authorial voice whilst constructing a text based on the texts of others. At the same time, such a programme implies a focus on authors, in order to move students towards an understanding of how knowledge is constructed.

I shall begin, therefore, with the negotiation of shared meaning and the development of policy, as a starting point for curricular intervention.

Negotiating shared meaning and developing policy: *The Taming of the Shrew*

The role of referencing: *a whirling dervish*

The voices in Part II show clearly that there are conflicting understandings about the role of referencing in the undergraduate curriculum, between students and their teachers, and amongst the academics themselves. Some academics see little sense in it at the undergraduate level. One lecturer did see an important role for referencing, yet most of the students on this lecturer's course who were interviewed did not seem to have a like grasp of this role, and were far from convinced of its significance.

As discussed in Part I, genre theorists such as Cope and Kalantzis (1993) and Kress (1985) make a plea for the explicit teaching of powerful written genres. The academic essay/article is one such powerful genre, as it is crucial to access and success for almost all students, as well as for those all-important publishing records of academic staff. In order to present the genre explicitly, those who teach need to bring to the surface their sometimes subliminal understanding of how the genre operates, its rules and its intricacies, and examine why they approach it in the way that they do. At best this is a process which happens jointly amongst academic staff within a department, so that emerging from discussions around the principal genre(s) of that discipline, policy and coherent teaching approaches may be developed. Within this framework, then, what the role of referencing is in the undergraduate essay needs to be discussed and debated. This debate should also include a consideration of the fit between the writing genres required within the curriculum and the predicted kind of workplace that students of a particular faculty or course may enter. This of course cannot be approached simplistically, not only because it is not possible to predict fully the genres that students will use in the workplace, but also because the academic essay assignment is a pedagogic genre, a tool for learning. However, as most students do not proceed to postgraduate studies, adequate preparation for economic empowerment in the world outside the institution must be a foundational consideration of the entire curriculum.

Once some shared understanding about the rationale for citation in academic writing has been reached between academic staff, this understanding can then be communicated to students. A useful way of penetrating the role and social function of documentation might be to approach the problem of plagiarism and referencing from the framework of different genres. If students are presented with a variety of kinds of documentation, such as in the novel, the speech, the newspaper article and the academic essay, and asked to think about why each is different, and the functions that each has in society, they may come to an understanding of referencing as taking part in the academic conversation, as locating intellectual traditions and schools of thought, and authors within them, and begin to think of themselves as authors who are part of that conversation. Copyright could also be broadly explored by thinking about its function in society. Whose interests do copyright laws protect, and who does not benefit? Interesting would be a discussion of how there is no copyright in ideas, although plagiarism can mean the use of ideas without acknowledgement. Why does this distinction exist? Crucial to an understanding of the role of referencing is an understanding of how knowledge is constructed, and how texts are authored. I shall discuss this more fully in the final part of this conclusion.

In order to communicate to students and tutors a rationale for referencing and rules for monitoring plagiarism, clear written definitions and policies need to be developed, both institutional and departmental.

Institutional policy

In a general discussion about academic dishonesty as a student development issue, Kibler (1993) stresses the importance of the development of clearly written policy, which should include 'definitions of academic dishonesty, examples of behaviours that constitute infractions, a description of the process followed when alleged violations occur, and a description of the sanctions usually imposed' (263). An institutional policy needs to contain a clear definition of what constitutes plagiarism, an acknowledgement of the complexities of this concept, general guidelines for academic staff on how to recognize and handle plagiarism, and for students on how to avoid it. It also needs to lay out clear disciplinary procedures for cases of intentional fraud. Usually institutional policy consists of the latter, but is not as clear on what plagiarism is or on how to handle or avoid it.

At the University of Cape Town, the 1995 General Rules for Students booklet simply contains a clause under 'academic conduct' which states the following:

> RCS 2.4. In any examination, test or in respect of the completion and/or submission of any other form of academic assessment, a student shall refrain from dishonest conduct. Dishonest conduct includes plagiarism or submission of the work of a person other than the student who is being examined.

(33)

Clearly this does not constitute a policy, as it contains neither definition, guidelines nor disciplinary procedures, though departmental handbooks usually warn students that they could be excluded from the university if they plagiarize. It is significant, however, that plagiarism is only seen as 'dishonest conduct'; there is no other possible explanation for it. Students everywhere are often warned about the consequences of plagiarism, which may be expulsion from the university, as well as the possibility of career opportunities being limited, or professional licensing being denied if there is a record of cheating in academic work. These are dire consequences indeed, and students need to know about them.

So any university administration needs to state clearly the possible consequences of an academic offence such as plagiarism. However, it also needs to indicate to students and staff that there are varying levels of plagiarism, and varying reasons for plagiarism, most of which are not 'cheating' or intentionally fraudulent. Whilst not condoning these, there should be some acknowledgement of them in policy guidelines. Howard (1995) has drafted an excellent institutional policy on plagiarism which could be successfully adapted to most contexts, and I shall summarize it briefly here, whilst recommending that those readers interested in institutional policy consult the full text. She insists that when institutions (as is common) only provide for disciplinary, juridical responses to plagiarism, they leave little room for a pedagogical response. Also, when universities describe plagiarism only in moral terms as 'academic dishonesty', they exclude the possibility not only of a lack of knowledge of the conventions of referencing, but also that there may be positive, 'commendable' reasons for what she calls 'patchwriting' (797). In addition, if a student plagiarizes, we need to know if the plagiarism was intentional or not, and if it was intentional, we need to know the student's motivation, and to take the educational context into account. Taking the context into account means finding out how experienced that student is in the disciplinary discourse, whether she/he has been taught proper citation conventions, and what the disciplinary expectations are regarding citation and tolerance of some forms of plagiarism, as these vary widely. Howard also introduces the reader as a crucial part of the context, confirming what Part II of this book has shown clearly: that plagiarism is differently interpreted across readers as well as within one reader's responses to different writers. She gives advice and examples for students, as well as advice for faculty.

Howard's definition of plagiarism divides it into three forms: cheating, non-attribution, and patchwriting. The first is deliberate fraud and the second usually stems from inexperience with citation conventions. Patchwriting is when a source has been too closely paraphrased, and is plagiarism regardless of whether the source has been acknowledged or not. Howard's policy on patchwriting is worth quoting here:

> patchwriting can actually help the learner begin to understand the unfamiliar material. Yet it is a transitional writing form; it is never acceptable for final-draft academic writing, for it demonstrates that the writer does not fully understand the source from which he or she is patchwriting.
>
> (799)

Thus an institutional policy should acknowledge the complexities of plagiarism, whilst at the same time not condone it as a writing strategy. It should make clear to academic staff that plagiarism is not always a negative, immoral act, may be symptomatic of underlying problems, and may provide a way in for an educator to understanding where these problems lie. The policy should exemplify possible reasons for plagiarism. Allowing academics to think of plagiarism differently will open pedagogical space for teachers to assist students in developing their authorial voices.

Departmental policies and models

The departmental handbook remains for some students the first and only place where they will receive guidelines, policies and definitions on plagiarism and models of citation practices and thus is an important pedagogical interface. The departmental handbook can also represent the genres and citation practices of the discipline, which an institutional policy cannot. I would like to make some practical suggestions of what might be included in a section on plagiarism and referencing in a departmental handbook.

Definitions. First, it seems to me to be crucial that a clear definition of what constitutes plagiarism is set out in a handbook for students. Central to definitional problems, as discussed in Chapter 3, is whether plagiarism occurs only when there is deliberate intention to deceive, or whether it also occurs simply with unintentional use of the words or ideas of others without acknowledgement. This is an important difference in definition, and a decision needs to be made on which definition is pedagogically appropriate at the undergraduate level, as there are important implications for how plagiarism is handled by markers. Intention to *deceive*, also, is different from intention to *imitate*, which may be a strategy for which the student has little alternative in the early stages of tertiary education.

Another definitional problem concerns the use of the *ideas* of others without acknowledgement, especially ideas presented in lectures, and whether this constitutes plagiarism at first-year level. Again, it is important that there is clarity on this issue, and that a clear statement is made about this in the handbook. I think that it may be important to indicate to students in a written policy that some areas are grey ones, and give them some pointers on what to do with such problems as:

- What constitutes common knowledge?
- What should the writer do with Bazerman's (1995: 357) 'deep sources' of knowledge? (i.e. 'those ideas and information that you came across long before you began work on the essay in question' which 'may be so far in the back of your memory that there is no way to identify which writers helped shape your thinking with respect to your current project').
- Is it appropriate to use ideas presented in lectures? Should these be acknowledged, and if so, how?
- If the lecture notes are written up and 'published' informally for student use, how should the use of these be acknowledged?
- What should be done about ideas developed orally, in conjunction with others, particularly where the 'origins' of these ideas are not clear?

Policy guidelines for markers. Secondly, it is essential that there is a clear policy guideline for markers on an appropriate response when plagiarism is suspected. I do not think that it is practical that every source used should be checked. I do think, however, that a clear message of disapproval in a low mark can be given, but with a route opened to the student to consult with the marker, and to be given the opportunity to rewrite the assignment. Even where there is intentional dishonesty in the form of plagiarism (and, to reiterate, my argument in this book is that this is not the principal form of 'plagiarism'), it is important that the opportunity be given to the student to discuss the ethical implications of his or her behaviour. Kibler (1993) reports on several studies which indicate that fear of failure and incompetence may result in dishonest behaviour, and advises against simply giving a failing grade to such students, as 'the practice does not serve as a deterrent for students already in jeopardy of failing' (264). Where it is an academic literacy problem of the kinds demonstrated in Part II, it is even more important that the student be given the opportunity to consult with the marker about the problems in the essay. Students should be encouraged to move towards a development of their own voice in academic writing, and I shall return to this later.

Models. The third consideration is the way in which appropriate referencing is illustrated in a departmental handbook. A first-year handbook at UCT (chosen for comment here because it is typical) gives a series of examples of how to reference, with a general rule preceding the example:

> References *usually* include page numbers and *must* include page numbers when the reference is to a direct citation. This can be either:
> a) How the Africans experienced the negation of their historical process and the distortion of their classes is described by Rodney (1972: 246)
> OR:
> b) Expropriations, taxation, corvees and paternalist control were conscious instruments of policy that created the needed labour force. (Murray, 1962: 121)

I think it is essential to give models of suitable citation practices, and this example is one of a range of illustrations of referencing. I would like, however, to propose an alternative, more contextualized way of demonstrating referencing. I think it might be helpful to include extracts from, for example, two sources on the same topic, with an acceptable paraphrased synthesis of the two, in order to demonstrate how they can be woven together with appropriate signals, and with the writer's own connections made between the two. All the different kinds of examples usually portrayed in isolated sentences may be demonstrated in this way, but within continuous discourse, so that there is a demonstration not only of how to signal the voices of others, but also how to signal one's own voice in an appropriate way, and within a meaningful context. Following this synthesis (or placed around the text with pointers) *an explanation for each reference* should be included – *why* it is appropriate to reference at each point. Where there are a number of sentences or a paragraph with no references, the reasons for this should also be explained. For instance, the problem of what constitutes common knowledge could be introduced in this way, as could ways of bringing in one's own ideas and linking them to those of the sources, as well as the question of what constitutes acceptable paraphrase. It might also be important to include some technical terms which cannot easily be substituted in a paraphrase. Students writing in an additional language would benefit from the inclusion in this text of several different examples of phrases which, first, introduce authors (such as 'according to', 'the position taken by'), secondly, link sources together ('X concurs with this view, but takes it further), and, thirdly, signal the writer's own voice ('I wish to argue', 'It seems that') and so on. These could then be drawn to the attention of the student reader by extracting and listing them under the three categories which I have mentioned (signalling other authors, linking sources, introducing one's own viewpoint). The optimal model would incorporate some examples and explanation of authorial stance, such as how to express tentative agreement, neutrality, etc. These are all ways of 'animating' the voices of others, so that the student as agent 'lives' within the sources she/he uses. Like the doll Coppélia who 'comes alive' when Swanhilde dances, the students need to animate their 'dead' papers, put their selves into their writing, and move away from being puppets to the Dr Coppelius figures of their sources.

The next step I consider to be essential. In order for space to be opened for discussion and dialogue, there needs to be difference. As a contrast, another synthesis of the same two sources should be modelled, with inappropriate paraphrase and referencing, or lack of referencing, overuse of quotation, etc., with some explanation again on why these examples are inappropriate. I shall consider the pedagogical usefulness of providing good and poor models for discussion with students in the second part of this conclusion.

Mediation of policy and models. The suggestions given above, of definition, policy and contextualized examples, could serve as an important framework for discussion about citation and plagiarism for lecturers and tutors, and for their marking, and as an important reference point for students while writing assignments and essays. I wish to emphasize that such definitions, policies and models require discussion and mediation, as placing them in a handbook will never be sufficient. Moreover, further examples of problematic as well as appropriate referencing or its absence need to be extracted from students' own writing and discussed in an ongoing manner with students within their curriculum.

The next section focuses on the need for us to examine marker assumptions regarding plagiarism, and the need for policy to be developed in order to diminish the negative effect of such assumptions.

The consequences of problematic assumptions about background knowledge and language ability: *Odette or Odile?*

Markers' practices in detecting plagiarism

The evidence in Part II suggests that the way in which the practice of referencing is enforced by some markers of essays can rest on problematic assumptions about the amount of background knowledge, which Bazerman (1995) calls 'deep sources', which different kinds of students bring to the topic of their writing. Related to this, markers' practices in detecting plagiarism rely on judging sophistication of language and sophistication of ideas, and where a student is a speaker of another language, expectations of what constitutes sophisticated language or ideas for that student may be lower. Pennycook (1996: 203) notes the irony in the notion of teachers searching for evidence of grammatical errors to discount their suspicion of plagiarism. The marker's modus operandi may generally not lead to incorrect assumptions, but the possibility is there, and evident in Part II in the cases of Tshediso and Mangaliso, who, for complex reasons, are not seen as legitimate users of 'deep sources' or outside sources, in the way that Laura and Emma are. In Bourdieu's (1991) terms, Tshediso and Mangaliso have not been 'authorized' to speak, they are seen as 'impostors', they are the Odiles of Swan Lake, and, though dancing brilliantly, they cannot be the real Odette, because their tutu is the wrong colour! Again for complex reasons, Mangaliso is given the benefit of the doubt regarding suspected plagiarism, and may demonstrate his legitimacy, while Nothando is denied this opportunity.

Access to background knowledge and learning theory

The 'shutting out' of student background knowledge in their writing, mainly by tutors, who require students to reference 'deep sources', has important implications within constructivist learning theory, and within writing-to-learn theory. Constructivist learning theory stresses the importance of access to background knowledge for the learner, in order for new knowledge to be built into the old framework. By relating new knowledge to what he or she already knows, the learner is using established knowledge to organize and make sense of the new, and, in so doing, the existing cognitive construction may shift in order to accommodate the new. Vygotsky's (1987) theories of language and concept development clarify how concepts change and develop through mediation, and so it is evident that it is crucial for the learner to be able to work with their present understandings in order for these to develop further.

There is little doubt that writing plays a crucial role in helping students learn (see, for example, Langer and Applebee, 1987). However, when students are not able to integrate what they know already with what they are learning in their writing, when they are denied their means of making sense of what they are learning through bringing themselves and what they know to the writing, we may in fact be hindering their learning processes. Not being allowed to bring his subjectivity to his writing, Tshediso constructed a split between reading and writing, which he described as 'I become subjective, I get involved to understand it, but now if I have to reproduce it, I read it again, and become objective, like a spectator.' This worked for him because he had realized that 'what I have to say, in comparison to what I have read, what I've read in fact carries more weight'. Tshediso's development in learning academic discourse meant a loss of some of the old authorities, as well as a deep struggle to maintain a sense of himself in his writing.

The quote from Thesen's (1997) student is worth repeating here:

> I don't feel really free in expressing my views. I just don't. . . . Sometimes you come up with what you feel is your personal feeling and then you're told that you're plagiarizing some White guy who happened to be fortunate to get information and to jot it down, not because you're stealing his ideas . . . it really limits us.
>
> (502)

So not legitimizing the background knowledge of the student may alienate him or her, causing disengagement from the topic, which can only be owned by 'some White guy' who wrote the ideas down. Instead of encouraging the incorporation of the writer's own ideas, in his or her own words, the inappropriate monitoring of plagiarism actually encourages what it purports to condemn: the parroting of sources, though acknowledged, and discourages what it purports to protect: 'originality' of ideas.

Use of sources not prescribed

In addition to this disallowing (in some cases) of student background knowledge and its implications for limitations on learning and 'original' thought, another consequence of false assumptions about students may be suspicion of plagiarism where students have used a source unknown to the marker, leading to a catch-22[1] situation where, although students are explicitly encouraged to go beyond the prescribed reading, if they do so they may be suspected of plagiarism. This is not to say that the deceitful student might not wilfully attempt such a ruse, but where a marker suspects but is unable to prove plagiarism, the possibility exists that the student has used and documented the unknown source appropriately. Again the student whose first language is not Eglish is more vulnerable than others to such incorrect assumptions, and the consequence of such an experience may be to remain scrupulously within the limits of the prescribed readings, as did Tshediso.

It is not my intention to criticize the often very careful processes of judgement undertaken by markers of assignments in evaluating the misuse of sources: I am aware of how delicate a process it is. My intention is simply to posit the possibilities and consequences of incorrect assumptions which were evident in Part II. To return to the words of Pennycook (1994), working in the context of Hong Kong, with Chinese students studying at Western, English-medium universities, who warns:

We need to be very cautious here of acting prejudicially against students, especially students who are not writing in their first language, because we assume their knowledge and linguistic skills are not sufficient to have produced a particular idea or phrase.

(282)

The problem of incorrect assumptions is exacerbated when there is no clear policy about checking of outside sources, and, where this is not possible, of how to deal with suspected plagiarism. In this research, the inconsistencies within one marker's approach to plagiarism emerged clearly, where one student was allowed to defend himself against the accusation of plagiarism, and another was not, a perhaps inevitable consequence of the absence of policy and discussion of policy. Also evident are substantial differences across markers in the thoroughness of referencing they require, in what they want documented, and what would be acceptable as common knowledge. It emerges in the research that this can be due to two factors: first, a difference in the way that markers approach referencing, and, secondly, the individual authority of the student, so that a student who writes with authority is expected to reference less thoroughly than the one who writes with less authority. It follows from this, once again, that clear definitions and policies need to be developed, written and discussed with tutors and students. It also follows that further research needs to be undertaken into what exactly constitutes authority in writing, and how this authority is established. With a clearer understanding of what authority in writing means, we might have a pedagogical starting point (and end point) for writing in the curriculum. I shall return to the nature of this authority in the final section of this conclusion.

Having dealt with what might be called 'preconditions' within the curriculum, I move on now to the second section of this conclusion, in which a developmental approach to referencing as a problem of academic literacy is set out.

Plagiarism and referencing within an academic literacy framework

The genres of the academy must be taught within the curriculum. Gee's (1990) use of the distinction between acquisition and learning is pertinent here. He defines acquisition as 'a process of acquiring something subconsciously by exposure to models, a process of trial and error, and practice within social groups, without formal teaching'. Learning, on the other hand, is 'a process that involves conscious knowledge gained through teaching ... or through certain life-experiences that trigger conscious reflection' (146). In order to perform in a discourse, we need to acquire it, by means of an apprenticeship to those who already know the discourse. In order to be able to talk about a discourse, we need to learn it, through conscious, explicit knowledge about that discourse. He explains that one needs both in a class-room, but that acquisition must come before learning, at least in part. Inter-estingly, Vygotsky's views on learning seem to contradict this sequence. For Vygotsky (1987) 'scientific' or schooled concepts develop *ahead* of 'everyday' concepts, because explicit instruction facilitates awareness, and awareness facilitates learning. I think that this is the part that Gee misses: learning actually facilitates acquisition and vice versa, the two modes interact and affect one another. It is therefore necessary to have explicit instruction about writing built into any academic curriculum, whilst at the same time appren-ticing learners to the genres of the discipline through their immersion in its discourses. Drawing on the research findings, I shall now discuss the unfamiliar nature of the genres of academy for most new students, and then move on to some of the things which need to be built into any writing-within-the-disciplines curriculum in order to effectively tackle the problems of plagiarism and appropriate citation practices.

The academic essay as a new genre: *dancing to a distant drum*

The simple analysis of students' past writing experiences presented in the Appendix shows clearly how writing from multiple sources is an entirely new activity for almost all the students interviewed, let alone referencing those sources, of which all the students had had no experience whatsoever. The dominant writing experience which these students had (and as the group included students from all kinds of educational backgrounds, it seems reasonable to conclude that this is the general South African experience) seems to be the narrative or descriptive composition, while a few have used one authoritative textbook in order to write an essay. This means that many students have had very little experience of working with a text and putting it into their own words. One student actually mentioned that in writing 'factual' essays at school you would fail if you did not reproduce the book as is. The school experience in other countries will be somewhat different, but, all over, the genres of the academic disciplines will be more or less new to the entering student. So it is partly a matter of simply not knowing how to do it, not knowing how to write in these genres in an appropriate way, because they have not been taught, neither their forms nor their functions.

Several students in the interviews also reported significant relationships to religious texts, which would encourage a reverent approach to sources, and discourage criticism and dispute. It is evident, therefore, that the prior literacy practices of many students do not support the discourses of the tertiary institution. A fundamental element of this, and an important source of citation problems, is the comprehension of and approach to texts. I shall deal with the comprehension first, and then move on to the approach to texts, though the two are interrelated.

Reading and reshaping

Although I did not focus on reading and note-taking in Part II, I would like to touch on it here. Many of the students who referenced inappropriately were simply using highlighters or underlining on the original texts as they read, and taking no notes. Alternatively they used the authors' words in their notes because they distrusted their own ability to represent those authors accurately. Those who presented well-referenced, well-synthesized essays took notes which reshaped the original text entirely, and indicated the sources in the notes. Reshaping the original is a high-order skill requiring excellent comprehension of the original text, and also the complex skills of paraphrase and summary. The very act of reshaping leads to comprehension, which is what lecturers who mark look for: the student who displays understanding through the use of examples and their own words.

This suggests, first, that careful selection of course readings needs to be made, not only for content but also for comprehensibility, and, secondly, that many students need a great deal of instruction and practice in comprehension strategies, paraphrase and summary techniques. Particularly useful in comprehension and summary is the use of concept or cognitive mapping, because of the necessity for reshaping and categorizing while summarizing, and because it can form a diagrammatic synthesis of what has been read (Novak and Gowin, 1984). Opportunities for learning these skills need to be built into the curriculum.

To turn now briefly to the approach to text. Here lies a complex cluster of problems of relationship to text, of an approach to learning inculcated in the schools, of a rigid notion of knowledge as a set of facts to be absorbed. Referencing interacts with these underlying contextual problems: difficulties with citation, and plagiarism, may be manifestations of these problems, while a focus on the fundamentals of referencing may make positive contextual and conceptual shifts in the minds of learners, as was evident in Tshediso's development over the year. I shall discuss this further when considering the question of what constitutes authority in writing.

The next section deals with a different order of problem, where the linguistic and conceptual resources are not available to the student, and he or she has no choice but to lean on the text.

Learning language and academic discourse by imitation

Learning to dance is all about watching and copying, watching and copying. The novice dancer needs more time to watch and copy. The novice writer of academic discourse, particularly the second-language speaker, such as Bulelwa, may need to cling closely to the original texts, because she has little linguistic resources at this stage for successful paraphrase, and because she is learning by imitation. Slowly the dancer begins to remember the sequence of steps, and no longer has to copy the dance teacher demonstrating the sequence: it begins to hold a place in her memory. Plagiarism in a context of learning an additional language can mean the reuse of chunks of language which have been stored in memory, an essential part of any language learning process.

In addition, language is intensely social, as I attempted to establish in Part I through the theories of Bakhtin (1981) and Kress (1985), amongst others. Of necessity we all learn and take language from those around us, and all texts are deeply contextualized in the discipline to which the novice writer is apprenticed. At the level of entrance into academia, learning a new discourse requires 'trying on' that discourse: stepping into the shoes of the authors. Hull and Rose (1990) discuss a nursing student, Tanya, who copies her source texts, changing a few words here and there, conscious of the problem of staying too close to the text, but unable to do anything else. Bulelwa too, was conscious of plagiarism, saying that 'by paraphrasing I don't want to plagiarize'. However, she was unable to do anything more than 'look at synonyms of the words', using the dictionary, a strategy which is not sustainable throughout an eight-page essay. Hull and Rose conclude that what Tanya needed was 'a freewheeling pedagogy of imitation, one that encourages her to try on the language of essays like the nurse's case study', with a gradual introduction of coherence markers and signals of the use of the words of the text (242). Lindiwe, on the other hand, knew the signals that need to be used to indicate quotations, but her strategy was to overuse quotation (she is what Howard (1995) calls a 'patchwriter'). Her thoughts were that if she put something into her own words, she would misrepresent the author, and that would be a more serious problem than patchwriting. I think here of Bakhtin's description of how words 'put themselves in quotation marks against the will of the speaker' and 'sound foreign in the mouth of the one who has appropriated them and now speaks them' (1981: 294). The words of the discourse are too socially and conceptually distanced from the writer for her to reshape them in any way, and she does not have the confidence in her language ability to even try. Such students need time to absorb and acquire the new discourses of the academy, as well as constructive pedagogical interventions that focus on explicit comprehension strategies, paraphrase and summary, and legitimate ways of representing their own and the voices of others.

Tshediso's effective use of my own assignment, which I had given him to read as a model for his own writing and use of sources, leads me to a simple conclusion: students need to see and discuss models of good essays and how sources are used within them, as well as poor essays which demonstrate inappropriate referencing strategies or plagiarism. Charney and Carlson (1995), in an experimental study to determine the impact of supplying writing models on students' writing of research texts, found that the group given models produced writing that was better organized, at the level of the sentence, paragraph, and overall structure, and conclude that model texts 'are a rich resource that may prove useful to writers in different ways at different stages of their development' (116). They also found that providing students with good, moderate and poor models may help students to develop a sense of effective and ineffective kinds of writing, and so increase their own effectiveness in writing. *How to use a model* needs to be part of a discussion of model texts, and giving students models of perhaps a previous, already completed essay for discussion will help to avoid the problem of inappropriate use of models. Another possibility is making copies of the best essay available to students for scrutiny. Again, if this essay is known to markers, it will be difficult for students in the following year, even if the topic stays the same, to use it inappropriately.

Having looked at the ways in which students learn through imitation, I turn now to a consideration of how they can be assisted in moving away from a tight dependence on the voices of others, to a situation where they begin to write with themselves as author/agent animating the voices of others.

Detecting and developing authorial voice

Voice detection in reading will facilitate voice development in writing. The dancer has to be able to hear the different instruments of the orchestra, the different strands of melody weaving through the music, the rhythms, discords and harmonies, in order to understand all aspects of that music. The richer the understanding of the music, the richer the possibilities for interpretation. Likewise in a reading, the student writer needs to be able to 'hear' where the sources agree and disagree, when the author is favouring the opinions of one source rather than another, when it is the author putting forward their ideas rather than stating the ideas of others. So as a first step, students need to be assisted in recognizing multiple voices in their reading. Giving students readings of original key theorists, and then examining how their work has been discussed and interpreted may be helpful (e.g. first Derrida and then X on Derrida). Allowing students to read the original sources will give them a sense of the first explication of the theories which so many have since interpreted, and they may then be better able to recognize the authorial stances of these interpretations in their further reading. The benefits of examining the original texts need to be weighed up against the comprehensibility of these texts.

Another consideration is whether prescribing a textbook is a useful way of getting students to understand the multivoiced nature of texts, and how knowledge is constructed and contested. Textbooks often contain far fewer references than journal articles, and tend to 'mute' and 'flatten' the voices of the sources from which they are drawn, often presenting authorial constructions as 'fact'.

To turn now to authorial voice in writing: often unnoticed in the emphasis on how to represent the voices of others is the problem of how to represent one's own voice amongst the voices of the authorities. The student interviews have highlighted this problem for me in three ways: first, the difficulty of legitimate representation of 'deep sources', i.e. previously stored background knowledge which is so deeply assimilated that there is no way of knowing the original source. The use of such knowledge should be encouraged and not shut out by the requirement that all information must be referenced. Secondly, the problem of how to present independent ideas developed by the novice student, which may be quite sophisticated, in such a way that plagiarism is not assumed. Related to this is the third problem of how to develop the subtle linguistic skills which are needed to indicate for the reader when the voice of the author is speaking, and what the authorial relationship is to what is being reported. An additionl complicating factor here is the use of indirect speech instead of quotation. Often the end of a paraphrase is indicated simply by a forward shift in modal auxiliary; again this may be difficult for the non-native speaker to detect or to use effectively in their writing.

Thus not only is the authorial stance of the writer in the readings given to students difficult to detect for the second-language learner, a difficulty which emerges in referencing problems in the essay, but also it seems to be exceedingly difficult for students to clearly indicate where the voices of others end and their own begins, if their own is present at all. 'Sampling is not so much ransacking the past as reanimating it', writes David Sanjek (1994: 352) of the practice of sampling in music. Authorship, too, means 'reanimating' and extending what has gone before. Where there is no authorial voice present, the writing is uninhabited. Although the novice writer may need to silently occupy the abodes of other writers for a while, at first simply absorbing the surroundings, it is important that they gradually begin to *live* within those abodes, that the reader of their writing has a sense of the occupant, because a sense of the occupant will also enhance the sense of the rooms that she or he occupies. In other words, an authorial voice animates the voices of others, and makes for a coherent, well-argued essay. Tshediso, despairing of ever doing this, saw his task after receiving feedback on his first essay as having to make a 'gallant attempt to write a dead essay', but felt an enormous satisfaction with his final Department P essay which he felt was a 'lively' paper which integrated the voices of many other writers. Tshediso, as author, began to move around in the academic abode of the discipline, to speak through the voices of others.

Permitting the use of the first person 'I' is an important way of encouraging an authorial voice. Writing about 'strains and strategies' in Political Science rhetoric, using an analysis of articles published in the *American Political Science Review*, Bazerman (1988) reports that the author in this discipline has a very active role in 'constructing ideas and collecting data as well as to claim credit for the research process and results' (287), and that this can be seen in the language in the use of the first person 'I' or 'we'. I think it would be fair to say that in almost all disciplines, even in the scientific and economic disciplines, the author is active in synthesizing research and constructing ideas and arguments. In the marking of essays, however, I saw instances of active disapproval of the use of the first person, particularly amongst tutors, and although using the first person is gaining ground in many journals, disapproval of 'I' in undergraduate writing seems, in places, to hold its ground. Allowing 'I' would certainly make the task of inserting the self as author into one's writing somewhat easier.

Collaborative writing practices, plagiarism and assessment

All dance requires interaction between many parts: choreographers, musicians, dancers. Just as copyright encourages the illusionary notion of the solitary author creating original text, the ethics of plagiarism and assessment practices in the tertiary institution discourage collaboration in writing. There is much evidence to support the richness and creativity inherent in collaborative writing and reading practices. Process-writing pedagogies make explicit use of collaborative processes of feedback and rewriting; Vygotskian learning theory exhorts that all learning is interactive. In the light of this, Lunsford and Ede (1994) call for a re-evaluation of testing and marking practices in higher education, which are all based on a notion of single authorship. Traces of collaborative work may be seen as plagiarism, and insistence on sole authorship forces the learner into a counter-educational mode of learning: the solitary. Creative forms of assessment which encourage and legitimize collaborative writing, at least at some points in the curriculum, are called for.

Referencing, authority and critical thinking

I turn now to the problem of particular, established approaches to text, and how a focus on authors can shift this approach. A complex cluster of problems huddles here, consisting of prior relationships to text, of an approach to learning inculcated in the school, of a rigid notion of knowledge as a set of facts to be learned.

A dancer with authority immediately draws the eye and stands out from the other dancers. It is hard to know what it is about this dancer that is compelling. Something to do with the fluidity of movement, something to do with a strong stage presence, much to do with technical strength, much to do with awareness of and communication with the audience, while remaining absorbed in the dance. I mentioned earlier that further research needs to be undertaken into what exactly constitutes authority in writing, and how this authority is established, within the text, as well as outside of it.

I suspect that this has to do with fluent language ability, an ease with the concepts and discourses of the discipline, and how the student projects herself or himself in tutorials, lectures and seminars. It also has to do with the wider society. In our still racially defined context in South Africa, sharp lines have been drawn historically between groups of people and the kinds of educational provision made for them. Furthermore, a historically 'white' university such as UCT still has a majority of white, male academic staff. I have not really touched on gender and class in this book; however, it is striking that most of the students struggling deeply with academic discourse that I interviewed were women from township or rural backgrounds. Also striking is that it was Nothando, a woman, and not Mangaliso, a man, who was *not* given the benefit of the doubt by S1, who marked both their essays. The women who were succeeding, such as Emma and Laura, were of privileged class and background. I do not wish readers to conclude from this that academic literacy problems relate only to certain groups of students. Although the depth of struggle is perhaps more evident in those from disadvantaged schooling, and whose first language is not English, and my concern is primarily with access to and success within the academy for these students, the academic essay is a new genre to almost *all* students, and any pedagogical provision that is made within the curriculum will have benefits for all students.

In any multiracial, gendered context, however, it may be that in Bourdieu's (1991) terms, authority is granted more easily to certain students, by those in positions of power, and withheld from others.[2] This may have a far-reaching impact: Mabizela (1994) notes how 'the impact of apartheid education can . . . be expressed in terms of different levels of confidence among different social groups. With particular reference to the field of education, black students are less confident about their knowledge and skills than their white counterparts' (24). Apartheid entrenched inequalities in all spheres of society, but such inequalities exist in all contexts beyond South Africa, though perhaps in more subtle forms.

Race/gender inequities in authority play themselves out in women and black students' lack of confidence in their own words and voices, and their overdependence on their sources.[3] Clark and Ivanic (1997) endorse this view, when discussing the writer's sense of their own authority, connected to their sense of power or status, which in turn is related to class, gender and ethnicity. They also see writer authority lying in 'how, and how far, writers appear authoritative by establishing an authorial presence in their texts' (152). Over-referencing may also be a sign of a lack of authority. It is at this point that it can become, as one lecturer termed it, 'a fetish which is engaged in to substitute thinking'. This insecurity was evident in the way that some tutors and lecturers (mainly women) talked about their own writing, and in the way that the tutors in particular marked. It was evident too in the students' writing, for instance in Lindiwe's overuse of quotation.

In a fascinating study of what constitutes authority in reading and writing, Penrose and Geisler (1994) studied the writing processes and products on the same topic of two writers, one a first-year student, the other completing his doctoral work in philosophy. Their study led them to 'four epistemological premises', which the doctoral student seemed to hold, but not the first-year student:

Texts are authored,
authors present knowledge in the form of claims,
knowledge claims can conflict,
knowledge claims can be tested.

(507)

The first-year student, Janet, did not reflect any of the authors in her draft of her essay, and her note-cards were labelled by topic rather than author, in contrast to the author-headed notes of the doctoral student. She saw 'the corpus of articles as a single definitive source rather than as a set of multiple voices in conversation' (509). For her, all the texts contained 'truths' and she saw her task as searching for facts. Where texts conflicted she was presented with a dilemma, choosing as a solution to report on only the position with which she agreed. She also saw no role for herself in her writing, and deliberately avoided inserting herself in any way, trying instead to present an 'objective' report of what she had read. Penrose and Geisler argue for

the role of rhetorical knowledge in the development of authority. In order for Janet to take authority in this or any other situation, she needs to believe there is authority to spare, that there is room for many voices. She needs to understand the development of knowledge as a communal and continual process.

(517)

They suggest more interactive models of education where a rhetorical perspective is 'enacted' (517), where students come to understand writers' processes and contexts in meaningful ways. They report on Greene (in Penrose and Geisler, 1994), who asks students to examine referencing practices and other discourse conventions in order to understand modes of disciplinary inquiry, and to begin to use these strategies themselves.

The evidence in Part II suggests that when a student focuses on referencing, in this case through Tshediso's reflection on referencing in interview discussions and journal writing, and begins to use it effectively, their understanding of the overall context of the discipline in which they are writing is enhanced. By this I mean their understanding of how knowledge is constructed, of the contexts of texts, and how they interrelate. Understanding how to locate knowledge through a location of authors within traditions and approaches develops through a focus on and understanding of the role of referencing. I would not claim that the focus on referencing is the only way in to such understandings, as probably the new understandings of knowledge construction are developing simultaneously through multiple processes, but I do believe that a deep understanding of the underlying rationale for referencing can lead to an understanding of how academic research is constructed upon the texts of others, of how authors are placed within the field, of how the academic debate takes place. The ability to adopt a critical stance, rather than present a set of 'truths' from the sources, may also develop through an understanding of sources as authored constructions which can be challenged and debated, especially with the support of other authorities in the field. (As Tshediso put it, if he wants to 'attack the views' of an author he needs to 'name' his 'opponent'.) A deep understanding of citation practices is a way in to all of Penrose and Geisler's epistemological premises: citation foregrounds authors, their claims and constructions, and how these conflict and are contested: it is a powerful way of helping to disestablish notions of received, absolute knowledge, and of developing a critical voice in students.

In conclusion, then, a pedagogy for plagiarism and referencing needs to begin with negotiation of shared meaning around the intricate problems of definition of plagiarism, in the context of the intensely social nature of language and cognition. It needs to move through the development of policy and demonstration materials as a reference point for practice and mediation within the curriculum. Finally, as the acquisition of academic discourses is often not supported by students' prior literacy practices or approaches to knowledge, and such acquisition can of necessity only occur within the academy, an appropriate pedagogy needs to approach plagiarism and referencing constructively, and developmentally, as a way in to an understanding of the nature of academic discourse and the construction of knowledge.

Notes

1. Hilary Janks, a reader of an earlier draft of this book, pointed out to me that no one would now think to source the phrase 'catch-22'.
2. The recent case in the media of alleged plagiarism by the Vice-Chancellor of Fort Hare, Professor Mzamane, and the struggles happening at the time of writing at the University of the Witwatersrand, over the alleged inaccurate curriculum vitae of the then newly appointed Deputy Vice-Chancellor, Professor Makgoba, vividly demonstrate the contestation occurring at the time around claims to authority.
3. The problem of lack of confidence leading to plagiarism has been discussed by Leibowitz (1994, 1995).

Appendix

Previous educational writing experience

The tables below represent an analysis of the previous educational writing experiences of the students interviewed, taken from interview data. They were responding to the question 'What kinds of writing did you do at school?' If they mentioned only creative writing in English, I would ask, 'And what about your other subjects?' If they mentioned something like 'factual writing', I would ask them how many sources they had been required to use.

Previous Educational Writing Experience of First-Year Students

Name	Education	'Factual' Writing		Comprehension	Letters	'Creative'
		one textbook	>1 source			
Mangaliso	(ex)DET[1] Franciscan Matric project	√	√		√	√
Lindiwe	(ex)DET	√				√
Bulelwa	Transkei	√		√		√
Nothando	(ex)DET			√		√
Busisiwe	(ex)DET	√				√
Tshediso	(ex)DET					√
Cathy	(ex)CED[2]	√		√		√
Laura	United World Colleges		√	√ (+lit. analysis)		

Noticeable in this table is the emphasis on 'creative' writing (by which most students seemed to mean narrative or descriptive compositions), mentioned by all except Laura, who was educated partly at the United World

Colleges (UWC) in Singapore. She is referring to this part of her education in this table. She is also one of only two who worked with more than one source when writing. She said that writing at the UWC was not much different from what she had to do at university, with a great deal of analysis and comparison, and that this was very different from what had been required of her at her previous CED school. Laura received 95% for her essay. The other person who had some experience of writing from multiple sources is Mangaliso, who attended a matric enrichment project run by Franciscans on the East Rand, and where apparently the teacher motivated students by giving them prizes for the best writing. None of the students interviewed had ever been expected to do anything like acknowledge their sources. Five of the students wrote essays using only one textbook as a source: the textbook was the authoritative body of facts. Several spoke of how the factual essay in history or biology was written in preparation for the examination where it would be reproduced.

The reports of the third-year students form a rather similar pattern, despite the differences in educational background.

Previous Educational Writing Experience of Third-Year Students

Name	Education	Writing done at school/previous ed. institution				
		'Factual' Writing		Comprehension	Letters	'Creative'
		one textbook	>1 source			
Carol	(ex)House of Representatives[3]					√
Veronica	A-levels Malawi	√				√
Emma	A-levels England Cambridge BA	√	√	√		√
Mandisi	Catholic School OFS					√
Sandy	Model C[4]					√
Themba	(ex)DET	√				√

Once again, 'creative' writing is the dominant form of writing in the schools attended by these students. Even the two students who did A-levels did not mention any writing from more than one source. The only experience of this is Emma's at Cambridge University where, as she said, she was never asked to reference. Themba went so far as to say that the factual writing had to come from the prescribed textbook – 'nothing else, otherwise you'll fail'. Themba was one of two who mentioned writing in another language, i.e. Xhosa, which he described as 'more analytical' than in English, where for instance a Xhosa proverb would be used as a stimulus for a piece of writing. Sandy also mentioned 'creative' writing in Afrikaans. A few students wrote poetry or personal essays or diaries, and Emma kept her diary of international political events.

Notes

1. School under the Department of Education and Training, formerly for African students only.
2. School under the Coloured Education Department, formerly for 'coloured' or mixed-race students.
3. School run by the former House of Representatives Education Department, formerly for Asian students only.
4. Formerly whites-only school which opened its doors to other races in the early 1990s.

References

Angélil-Carter, S. and Thesen, L. (1993). English for Academic Purposes within the institution: the shape of a shadow. In Angélil-Carter (ed.), *Language in Academic Development at U.C.T. 1993*. Academic Development Programme, University of Cape Town.

Angélil-Carter, S. and Hutchings, C. (1995a). Plagiarism: Academic theft or academic skill? *Monday Paper*, 14(24): 5.

Angélil-Carter, S. and Hutchings, C. (1995b). Plagiarism uncovered. *Monday Paper*, 14(28): 4–5.

Angélil-Carter, S. and Murray, S. (1996). An analysis of instances of academic discourse: Examining a departmental handbook. *South African Journal of Applied Language Studies*, 4(2): 15–31.

Angélil-Carter, S. (1997). Second language acquisition of spoken and written English: Acquiring the skeptron. *TESOL Quarterly*, 31(2): 263–87.

Atkinson, D. (1997). A critical approach to critical thinking in TESOL. *TESOL Quarterly*, 31(1): 71–94.

Bakhtin, M.M. (1981). *The Dialogic Imagination*. Austin: University of Texas Press.

Ballard, B. and Clanchy, J. (1988). Literacy in the university: An 'anthropological' approach. In G. Taylor, B. Ballard, V. Beasley, H. Bock, J. Clanchy (eds.), *Literacy by Degrees*. Milton Keynes: Society for Research into Higher Education & Open University Press.

Bannet, E.T. (1989). *Structuralism and the Logic of Dissent: Barthes, Derrida, Foucault, Lacan*. London: Macmillan Press.

Bartholomae, D. (1985). Inventing the university. In M. Rose (ed.), *When a Writer Can't Write*. New York: Guildford Press.

Bazerman, C. (1988). *Shaping Written Knowledge: The Genre and Activity of the Experimental Article in Science*. Madison: University of Wisconsin Press.

Bazerman, C. (1995). *The Informed Writer: Using Sources in the Disciplines*. Boston: Houghton Mifflin Company.

Bloch, J. and Chi, L. (1995). A comparison of the use of citations in Chinese and English academic discourse. In D. Belcher and G. Braine (eds.), *Academic Writing in a Second Language*. Norwood, NJ: Ablex.

Bloom, H. (1982). Plagiarism – a symposium. *Times Literary Supplement*, 9 April 1982: 413–15.

Bock, Z. and Winberg, C. (1993). Literary criticism and background knowledge: Readings of Oswald Mtshali's 'Reapers in a Mieliefield'. In S. Angélil-Carter (ed.), *Language in Academic Development at U.C.T. 1993*. Academic Development Programme, University of Cape Town.

Bourdieu, P. (1991). *Language and Symbolic Power*. Cambridge: Polity Press.

Bourdieu, P. and Passeron, J.-C. (1994). Introduction: Language and relationship to language in the teaching situation. In P. Bourdieu, J.-C. Passeron, and M. de Saint Martin, *Academic Discourse*. Cambridge: Polity Press.

Bowers, C.A. and Flinders, D.J. (1990). *Responsive Teaching: An Ecological Approach to Classroom Patterns of Language Culture and Thought*. New York: Teachers College Press.

Cazden, C.B. (1992). *Whole Language Plus: Essays on Literacy in the United States and New Zealand*. New York: Teachers College Press.

Charney, D.H. and Carlson, R.A. (1995). Learning to write in a genre: What student writers take from model texts. *Research in the Teaching of English*, 29(1): 88–125.

Chiseri-Strater, E. (1991). *Academic Literacies: The Public and Private Discourse of University Students*. Portsmouth, NH: Boynton/Cook Publishers.

Clark, R. and Ivanic, R. (1997). *The Politics of Writing*. London: Routledge.

Collins Dictionary of the English Language. 2nd edn. (1986), ed. P. Hanks and W.T. McLeod. London: Collins.

Concise Oxford Dictionary of Current English. 8th edn. (1992), ed. R.E. Allen. New York: Oxford University Press.

Cope, W. and Kalantzis, M. (1993). Introduction: How a genre approach to literacy can transform the way writing is taught. In W. Cope and M. Kalantzis (eds.), *The Powers of Literacy: A Genre Approach to Teaching Writing*. London: The Falmer Press.

Cummins, J. and Swain, M. (1986). *Bilingualism in Education*. Harlow: Longman.

Devitt, A.J. (1991). Intertextuality in tax accounting. In C. Bazerman and T. Paradis (eds.), *Textual Dynamics of the Professions*. Madison: University of Wisconsin Press.

Edelsky, C. (1991). *With Literacy and Justice for All: Rethinking the Social in Language and Education*. London: The Falmer Press.

Fairclough, N. (1992). *Discourse and Social Change*. Cambridge: Polity Press.

Feather, J. (1994). From rights in copies to copyright: The recognition of authors' rights in English law and practice in the sixteenth and seventeenth centuries. In M. Woodmansee and P. Jaszi (eds.), *The Construction of Authorship*. Durham, NC and London: Duke University Press.

Foucault, M. (1984). What is an author? In P. Rabinow (ed.), *The Foucault Reader*. Harmondsworth: Penguin.

Freedman, A. and Medway, P. (1994). Introduction: New views of genre and their implications for education. In A. Freedman and P. Medway (eds.), *Learning and Teaching Genre*. Portsmouth, NH: Boynton/Cook Heinemann.

Garson, P. (1995). Mzamane: Author in his own write? *Mail and Guardian*, 11–17 August: 8.

Gee, J. (1990). *Social Linguistics and Literacies: Ideology in Discourse*. Bristol: The Falmer Press.

Geisler, C. (1994). *Academic Literacy and the Nature of Expertise: Reading, Writing and Knowing in Academic Philosophy*. Hillsdale, NJ: Lawrence Erlbaum Associates.

Gere, A.R. (1994). Common properties of pleasure: Texts in nineteenth century women's clubs. In M. Woodmansee and P. Jaszi (eds.), *The Construction of Authorship*. Durham, NC and London: Duke University Press.

Giddens, A. (1987). Structuralism, post-structuralism and the production of culture. In A. Giddens and J. Turner (eds.), *Social Theory Today*. Cambridge: Polity Press.

Heath, Shirley Brice (1983). *Ways with Words: Language, Life and Work in Communities and Classrooms*. Cambridge: Cambridge University Press.

Howard, R.M. (1995). Plagiarisms, authorships, and the academic death penalty. *College English*, 57(7): 788–806.

Hull, G. and Rose, M. (1990). Toward a social-cognitive understanding of problematic reading and writing. In A.A. Lunsford, H. Moglen and J. Slevin (eds.), *The Right to Literacy*. New York: The Modern Language Association of America.

Jameson, D. (1993). The ethics of plagiarism: How genre affects writers' use of source materials. *The Bulletin*, June: 18–28.

Jaszi, P. (1994). On the author effect: Contemporary copyright and collective creativity. In M. Woodmansee and P. Jaszi (eds.) *The Construction of Authorship*. Durham, NC and London: Duke University Press.

Kibler, W.L. (1993). Academic dishonesty: A student development dilemma. *NASPA Journal*, 30(4): 253–67.

Kress, G. (1985). *Linguistic Processes in Sociocultural Practice*. Oxford: Oxford University Press.

Lakoff, G. and Johnson, M. (1980). *Metaphors We Live By*. Chicago: University of Chicago Press.

Langer, J.A. and Applebee, A.N. (1987). *How Writing Shapes Thinking: A Study of Teaching and Learning*. Urbana, Ill.: National Council of Teachers of English.

Lather, P. (1991). *Getting Smart: Feminist Research and Pedagogy With/in the Postmodern*. New York: Routledge.

Leibowitz, B. (1994). A revealing correspondence: Research into students' learning and writing in the first year History course. In M. Walker (ed.), *AD Dialogues 2*. Bellville: University of the Western Cape.

Leibowitz, B. (1995). Transitions: Acquiring academic literacy at the University of the Western Cape. *Academic Development*, 1(1): 33–46.

Lensmire, T.J. and Beals, D.E. (1994). Appropriating others' words: Traces of literature and peer culture in a third-grader's writing. *Language in Society*, 23: 411–25.

Lunsford, A.A. and Ede, L. (1994). Collaborative authorship and the teaching of writing. In M. Woodmansee and P. Jaszi (eds.), *The Construction of Authorship*. Durham, NC and London: Duke University Press.

Lunsford, A.A. and West, S. (1996). Intellectual property and composition studies. *College Composition and Communication*, October 1996.

Mabizela, M. (1994). Voices from first year students at UWC. In B. Leibowitz and M. Walker (eds.), *AD Dialogues 3*. Bellville: University of the Western Cape.

McCarthy, L.P. (1991). A psychiatrist using DSM-III. The influence of a charter document in psychiatry. In S. Bazerman and J. Paradis (eds.), *Textual Dynamics of the Professions*. Wisconsin: University of Wisconsin Press.

McEwan, I. (1982). Plagiarism – a symposium. *Times Literary Supplement*, 9 April: 413–15.

Mallon, T. (1989). *Stolen Words: Forays into the Origins and Ravages of Plagiarism*. New York: Ticknor and Fields.

Mellers, W. (1982). Plagiarism – a symposium. *Times Literary Supplement*, 9 April: 413–15.

Miller, K.D. (1993). Redefining plagiarism: Martin Luther King's use of an oral tradition. *Chronicle of Higher Education*, 20 Jan.: A60.

Moder, C.L. and Halleck, G.B. (1995). Solving the plagiary puzzle with role plays. *TESOL Journal*, 4(3): 16–19.

Mooney, C.J. (1992). Critics question Higher Education's commitment and effectiveness in dealing with plagiarism. *Chronicle of Higher Education*, 12 Feb.: A13–16.

Murphy, R. (1990). Anorexia: The cheating disorder. *College English*, 52: 898–903.

Novak, J.D. and Gowin, D.B. (1984). *Learning How to Learn*. Cambridge: Cambridge University Press.

Ong, W.J. (1982). *Orality and Literacy: The Technologizing of the Word*. London: Routledge.

Oxford Advanced Learner's Dictionary of Current English (1980). Ed. by A.S. Hornby. Oxford: Oxford University Press.

Peirce, B.N. (1995). Social identity, investment, and language learning. *TESOL Quarterly*, 29(1): 9–31.

Pennycook, A. (1994). The complex contexts of plagiarism: A reply to Deckert. *Journal of Second Language Writing*, 3(3): 277–84.

Pennycook, A. (1996). Borrowing others' words: Text, ownership, memory and plagiarism. *TESOL Quarterly*, 30(2): 201–30.

Penrose, A.M. and Geisler, C. (1994). Reading and writing without authority. *College Composition and Communication*, 45(4): 505–20.

Randall, M. (1991). Appropriate(d) discourse: Plagiarism and decolonization. *New Literary History*, 22: 525–41.

Recchio, T.E. (1991). A Bakhtinian reading of student writing. *College Composition and Communication*, 42(4): 446–54.

Reynolds, J. and de Klerk, V. (1998). Entering the discourses of the University. *South African Journal of Applied Language Studies*, 6(1): 43–58.

Rogers, P. (1982). Plagiarism – a symposium. *Times Literary Supplement*. 9 April: 413–15.

Rose, M. (1985). The language of exclusion: Writing instruction at the University. *College English*, 47(4): 341–59.

Rose, M. (1994). The author in court: *Pope vs. Curll* (1741). In M. Woodmansee, and P. Jaszi (eds.), *The Construction of Authorship*. Durham, NC and London: Duke University Press.

Sanjek, D. (1994). 'Don't have to DJ no more': Sampling and the 'autonomous' creator. In M. Woodmansee and P. Jaszi (eds.), *The Construction of Authorship*. Durham, NC and London: Duke University Press.

Scollon, R. (1994). As a matter of fact: The changing ideology of authorship and responsibility in discourse. *World Englishes*, 13(1): 33–46.

Scollon, R. (1995). Plagiarism and ideology: Identity in intercultural discourse. *Language in Society*, 24: 1–28.

Shay, S., Bond, D. and Hughes, T. (1995). Mysterious demands and disappointing responses: Exploring students' difficulties with academic writing tasks. In S. Angélil-Carter, D. Bond, M. Paxton and L. Thesen (eds.), *Language in Academic Development at U.C.T. 1994*. Academic Development Programme, University of Cape Town.

Sherman, J. (1992). Your own thoughts in your own words. *ELT Journal*, 46(2): 190–8.

Silverman, D. (1993). *Interpreting Qualitative Data: Methods for Analysing Talk, Text and Interaction*. London: Sage Publications.

Spack, R. (1997). The rhetorical construction of multilingual students. *TESOL Quarterly*, 31(4): 765–74.

Street, B.V. (1995). *Social Literacies: Critical Approaches to Literacy in Development, Ethnography and Education*. London: Longman.

Sutherland, J. (1982). Plagiarism – a symposium. *Times Literary Supplement*, 9 April: 413–15.

Swales, J.M. (1990). *Genre Analysis: English in Academic and Research Settings*. Cambridge: Cambridge University Press.

Thesen, L.K. (1994). Voices in discourse: Rethinking shared meaning in academic writing. Unpublished M.Phil. dissertation, University of Cape Town.

Thesen, L.K. (1997). Voices, discourse and transition: In search of new categories in EAP. *TESOL Quarterly*, 31(3): 487–511.

Thomas, M.W. (1994). Reading and writing the Renaissance Commonplace Book: A question of authorship? In M. Woodmansee and P. Jaszi (eds.), *The Construction of Authorship*. Durham, NC and London: Duke University Press.

University of Cape Town (1995). General Rules for Students. Published by the University of Cape Town.

Vygotsky, L.S. (1987). *Collected Works Vol 1*. Ed. R.W. Rieber and A.S. Carton. New York: Plenum Press.

Webster's New World Dictionary (1990). Ed. V. Neufeldt and A.N. Sparks. New York: Warner Books.

Weinert, R. (1995). The role of formulaic language in second language acquisition: A review. *Applied Linguistics*, 16(2): 180–205.

Wertsch, J.V. (1991). *Voices of the Mind: A Sociocultural Approach to Mediated Action*. London: Harvester Wheatsheaf.

Womack, P. (1993). What are essays for? *English Education*, 27(2): 42–9.

Woodmansee, M. (1994). The author effect: Recovering collectivity. In M. Woodmansee and P. Jaszi (eds.), *The Construction of Authorship*. Durham, NC and London: Duke University Press.

Woodmansee, M. and Jaszi, P. (1995). The law of texts: Copyright in the Academy. *College English*, 57(7): 769–87.

Yen, A.C. (1994). The interdisciplinary nature of copyright theory. In M. Woodmansee and P. Jaszi (eds.), *The Construction of Authorship*. Durham, NC and London: Duke University Press.

Index of authors

Index of terms

Lightning Source UK Ltd.
Milton Keynes UK
UKOW06f1722201115

263192UK00003B/179/P